# A Life Interrupted

## *By Tim Bransfield*

"I dedicate my story to my close friends, all of the therapists I have had, all patients I have met and to my entire family. They are the ones who have given me the support and encouragement I needed ever since my life changed forever on August 14, 2002."

*~Tim Bransfield*

# Introduction

I first met Tim Bransfield during the summer of 2014. We got together at a local eatery to talk in person about his upcoming book project. Across from me sat a young man full of life, brimming with enthusiasm, and ready to take on the world. As I came to know more of Tim's journey while working through his manuscript, I found it difficult to reconcile the young man who sat before me with the Tim you will soon read about. Such is the power of the human spirit to rise in the face of seemingly insurmountable hardship.

As a fellow traumatic brain injury survivor, I found myself identifying at every twist and turn in Tim's story. His writing style is in virtual lockstep with the Tim that I have come to know. He jumps ahead, circles back, takes a few detours along the way, yet he always manages to get back on track. I laughed, I cried and I have enjoyed every moment of working with Tim helping to bring his book to you. If you have a life that has been impacted in any way by a traumatic brain injury, your journey is about to be enriched.

*~David A. Grant*

# Foreword

*"To all people who have experienced a brain injury, the human spirit is stronger than anything that can happen to it. If there is a will, there is a way!"*

This quote that I wrote is on the dedication page of both of my books, *Coping with Mild Traumatic Brain Injury* and my recent book, *Concussion and Mild Traumatic Brain Injury: A Guide to living with the Challenges Associated with Post Concussion Syndrome and Brain Trauma.* Both I co-authored with Barbara Albers Hill.

Tim Bransfield's journey documented in this book truly reflects his spirit and determination to regain his life again. I first became aware of Tim's journey while reading our local newspaper, the *Tri Town Transcript* in 2002. The news article detailed Tim's accomplishments as a baseball player at our local regional high school, Masconomet. The article noted that Bransfield was the MVP of the Cape Ann League the previous spring as well as the MVP of the

Massachusetts vs. Connecticut game played at Fenway Park. The article went on to say that Tim, an All-Scholastic baseball player from Masconomet, was lying in a coma at Spaulding Rehabilitation Hospital following a major automobile accident.

What is wonderful about living in a rural area is the sense of real community and coming together to help one another. In the article there was a fund raising effort: Tim Bransfield Day, with all proceeds going to help pay for Bransfield's recovery and rehabilitation.

Deeply touched by the article and the support of the community, I felt compelled to call and offer my help in his recovery. I immediately picked up the phone and called the Bransfield home and explained that I was a neuropsychologist, who also had sustained a brain injury from a 60 mile-an hour head on automobile accident. I went on further to explain that I had developed a five prong approach to regain my life again, and that I wrote a book about it. One of the approaches that I mentioned was neurofeedback. This has changed my life completely. I explained that I was told by every doctor that I saw that I would never regain my life again. I had difficulty walking talking and thinking. On my neuropsychological testing, I was in the sixth percentile in the areas of deficit. Remarkably, after neurofeedback, I had progressed to the eightieth percentile.

Tim's mom thanked me at the time, yet emphasized he was still in a coma and that she appreciated the offer, call and support. Hanging up the phone, I wasn't sure if I would hear from them again, yet hoped that I could help. Then over a year later, in October of 2003, Tim started his journey with me and using neurofeedback to help him regain his life again. One of Tim's obstacles was his past history of seizures coupled with diet filled with junk food. The former was the easier to deal with, since there are medication and specific protocols in neurofeedback for seizure control. Changing Tim's diet and eating habits was a real challenge. He used to refer to me and my brain diet as being connected to the Devil.

At this point of his journey to regain his life, Tim could not remember what he ate only hours before. After several months of neurofeedback, Tim turned to his mother and questioned about what he had eaten earlier. This brought tears of joy into his mother's eyes. We were making progress. Over the next few months, Tim continued to improve, his spirit was always strong and by December 2003, Tim was more talkative and his short term memory continued to improve. He had been to baseball camp and did well. Tim's dream of going to Wheaton College was just on the horizon.

He did eventually go there, however, the American with Disability Act was not in full force and the college, was not equipped to help and truly assist Tim. Yet, this did it not dissuade Tim from his dream or break his spirit.

In this book, *A Life Interrupted,* you will read about Tim's journey from the darkness to the light. Tim is an inspiration to all to follow their dreams. One of the most amazing things that I have learned from Tim was my old misconception about loss memories. As noted above, Tim had both long-term and short-term memory problems. And from my training that any incoming information acquired during this period could not be sustained and definitely was not permanently registered.

Then one day, I walked into the office and told him I had met his previous speech and language pathologist. There was a time when Tim had virtually no recall of Amy Karas, who now works on my team of experts. Tim hearing her name said he totally remembered Amy and how they worked together. It was like Amy's name was the Rosetta Stone. I stopped Tim in mid-sentence, because I couldn't believe what I was hearing. I questioned if this was real or he was confabulating, which he never did. I immediately called both his mother and Amy on the phone and then told Tim to continue his recollection of Amy.

Both his mother and Amy were in tears on the phone and said that everything Tim was saying was accurate. This was truly the beginning of Tim being able to write this book, because he did remember. He remembered everything in detail after detail. Shocked by this experience, I reached out to other neuroscientists. How could this be true? How could you possibly recall information when at the time you could not recall even two words?

A Russian neuroscientist, Alexi Berd, is an international neuroscience librarian. He found research showing that every cell has a memory and given the proper stimulation, it can recall the information stored. We generally think of muscle memory, but here was factual information that was stored and hearing Amy's name was the key to waves and a flood of detailed memories that are now shared in this wonderful, inspirational book.

*Diane Roberts Stoler, Ed.D*

Neuropsychologist, Board Certified Health Psychologist, Board Certified Sports Psychologist, Brain Injury Survivor

# Chapter One

## The Night My World Forever Changed

*"If you're trying to achieve greatness, there will be roadblocks. I've had them; everybody has had them. But obstacles don't have to stop you. If you run into a wall, don't turn around and give up. Figure out how to climb it, go through it, or work around it."*

~Michael Jordan

My life changed forever on August 14, 2002. It was on that date that I sustained a traumatic brain injury. Much of what follows is a chronicle of my life since my injury. I share about the people I have met along the way as they all helped shaped me into the person I am today. Some of what I share has been on my mind for years but I've never had the opportunity to share – until now. I was fortunate as I didn't go through the hardest years of my life alone. No one going through a hard time should. The people I truly care for, the ones who mean the most to me were always there when I needed them.

One night changed my life, my world and everything in it. I was at a party at the house of an old high school teammate of mine. All my close high school friends were there. It was an exciting time. In a couple of weeks we would all be going to college and starting new lives. My girlfriend, Nicole, was not at the party. We were having an argument and it looked like we were going to break up before we left for college. But it was a great party and my friend Wayne drove me home around midnight. When I got home that night, I called Nicole right away. We started to talk about whether or not we should stay together. I wanted to see her and settle it face-to-face, and not over the phone. As she only lived a few miles away, I decided to go see her. I grabbed my keys and hopped into my car. I had a few drinks at the party and I struggled with getting the key into the ignition. I got frustrated and decided to go back inside to get my mother's keys to her car. Back inside the house my sister Michaella saw me.

"Tim, what are you doing?" She asked with obvious concern.

"I'm going to see Nicole" I replied.

"What do you mean you're going to see Nicole? You can't drive!"

She was yelling at me but I didn't listen to her. I gave my dog a pat goodbye and ran out of the house. I backed my mother's car out of the driveway slowly and silently so no one would hear. I felt a sigh of relief and was on my way.

I don't remember anything after that. My only memories are of what people later told me. I passed a police officer on my way to Nicole's. It was late, almost two in the morning and I had alcohol on my breath. The police officer turned around and started to follow me so I picked up speed. I do have a seizure disorder so it isn't clear if I was having a seizure when I drove into that tree or maybe it was the alcohol I had at the party or possible a combination of both. I hit the tree at eighty miles per hour. In an instant everything went dark.

I would spend the next sixty days in a coma. I thank God that police officer was there. If he wasn't close by I would not be alive today. It was like I took a break from life for three months starting on August 14, 2002. I say three months but it was really a much longer time than that.

Crashing into that tree changed my life forever. The first couple years after my brain injury, I battled with depression. My depression had me thinking about doing things to myself that I never thought of before. It was many years after I woke up when I started to accept my situation. The competitive fire was reignited inside of me.

I was taken to Beverly Hospital in an ambulance. My mother and father were notified by the police and they came right to the hospital. There was a priest there giving me my last rites but my mother threw him right out. She knew I wasn't going anywhere. Due to the seriousness of my injuries a decision was made to take me quickly to Beth Israel Hospital in Boston. Beth Israel is one of the best hospitals in Boston and that was proven by the wonderful Trauma Unit staff that treated me there. No one thought I would make it, including the EMTs. They wouldn't even let my mother in the ambulance on the trip down because of what might happen. My death seemed certain.

After arriving to Beth Israel, the trauma team gave my parents the thumbs up, meaning I was stable and still alive. My girlfriend Nicole came immediately to the hospital with her parents and sat with my parents in a small room, just waiting for some news. When they were finally allowed to see me they couldn't believe their eyes. I had blown up like a balloon and was just lying there hooked up to all kinds of medical equipment.

The next day a bunch of my friends came to the hospital to wait to see if I was going to make it. It was a big group – close to twenty-five friends and family. Some slept in the waiting room, while others came and went, but there was always someone there. Parents brought food in and everyone was there to get support from each other. After a couple of days a few of my very close friends and relatives were allowed to come in my room and see me. Some couldn't handle it and fainted. Such was the shape I was in.

Although I have no memory of this time, I've been told that my girlfriend Nicole was alongside me every minute until I came home. My mother tells me that she really needed Nicole there because she would ask the nurses questions about the medical equipment and knew when things needed attention. All my mother could do was to be there and hold my hand. Nicole and I had dated for about a year in high school. She was beautiful and a very good athlete. However it is still hard to remember being with her, but when I woke up I knew she was someone special in my life. She was always there and I was told she was my girlfriend. She was planning to go to Drexel University in Philadelphia to become an architect, but she didn't go that September. She chose not to leave my side. By the following February, she knew she had to get on with her life. It was a hard decision for her, I know. It was not easy hanging around with someone who kept repeating themselves and couldn't remember anything.

The funny thing was that I couldn't remember her breaking up with me. For quite a while I kept calling her, acting like everything was fine. When I finally realized she went her own way I was upset. Now I can see she did what she had to. I was no longer the Tim that she knew.

On September 23rd of 2002 I was well enough to be removed from the medical machines and was finally able to breathe on my own. It was at that time I was transferred to Spaulding Rehabilitation Hospital. I was 6'1" when I graduated from high school, went into my coma and woke up at 6'3". This was just one of the many surreal experiences of this new journey. My father grew six inches during his first year of college. My dad joked about it saying, "Your mother put you in the rack, I told her not to but she said that he's sleeping, he won't feel it."

The night of my brain injury I do not remember in the least, I am glad I don't. Every day of my life after that would prove to be a test of my mental and physical strength. I had no idea how different my life was about to be.

## Chapter Two

## My Pre-Accident Life

*"I've missed more than 9000 shots in my career. I've lost almost 300 games. 26 times I've been trusted to take the game winning shot and missed. I've failed over and over and over again in my life. And that is why I succeed."*

~Michael Jordan

My life before my brain injury was typical for children and young adults in my community. I grew up in the small town of Topsfield, Massachusetts. Topsfield is located about thirty minutes north of Boston. I lived in the part of the town that was perfect for a young kid to grow up in. My best friend lived right across the street from me. She came over to "play" every day. We stayed best friends all through school and I still consider Brooke my best friend today. She is kind of like my sister. She even calls my mother mom.

Her older sister Teal and my brother, Bobby, were always a part of what we did. When we would play house regularly. As Teal was the oldest, she was always the mother. Another game we would play was kind of like dominos with books. In my house I had two sets of stairs on each side and also lots and lots of books. Bobby and Teal went one way, putting the books up and Brooke and I went the other. Once everything was in place we tipped over one book and ran around trying to follow it and watch them all fall over, laughing the whole time. Some days we would set up a lemonade stand at the top of my driveway. We would only make a few quarters but it was good enough for us to go to the candy store down the street. I had a family video camera and we walked around my house filming all sorts of things.

Every day we would go over to see our neighbor Mrs. Jeffery. She lived alone, right through the woods in a small white house nearby. We all loved her and she loved having us around to come over and keep her company. We called her, "the cookie lady." Every day we knocked on her door and she would come to the front door with some of cookies to give us. Some days she let us in and we would be able to run around her house.

Tim was another friend and neighbor. We were in the same grade and we loved to play basketball. We also both idolized Michael Jordan. Tim was not into baseball that much but we had many other things in common that made us good friends. I am blessed as we are still good friends today.

During the winters I would walk through my back yard woods to his house and watch a basketball game or a movie. We would hang out in his basement and build forts with all his couch cushions and other things around his house. He had a bunch of Nerf guns. We would jump out from the side of the cushions and shoot each other with them.

His parents would always go out to dinner or go out with friends on Fridays and Saturdays so we had the house to ourselves most of the time. After playing downstairs we would come up to his kitchen. We took out the blender, some ice cream and many other things to make a shake. I don't know how good they were but at eight or nine years old, anything with ice cream is good!

During the school year Brooke walked across the street and Tim walked through the woods to the bus stop in front of my driveway. For me, no matter where I was I always had to be moving and doing something or I would get bored. When Tim got to the bus stop we would shoot baskets until the bus came. Brendan and Kevin, two other good friends, would join us. They both liked the same stuff we did and living so close to me that we quickly became good friends.

Because there were so many of my friends living close to me, on the weekends and almost every day in the summer we would play "man hunt." My back yard was very big and so was Tim's. It was easy to find places to hide and run away if we were found. A lot of our other friends from grade school, Todd, Chris, Nick, James and Mike were all part of this special time in my life. I am happy they are still good friends today.

In grade school everyone's favorite time during the day is recess. Someone always brought a basketball to school so during recess the first couple years that's what we would play.

By the end of grade school we switched it up. Someone started to bring in a mini football so we went to the outfield to play. No one wanted to play tag football because we were all too tough for that. After recess, almost every day, someone came back into school with some sort of injury. No one wanted to or liked to admit it, though. The best time to play football at recess was during the winter when it snowed and there was a little cushion to soften the blow when you were tackled.

During recess, by playing basketball and football everyone got to see who the good athletes were. I don't think anyone was thinking about what would happen when we got to high school and played, at least I didn't. We were all just having innocent fun.

I always wanted to play baseball at recess but that might have been too hard and maybe too dangerous for everyone. Someone could get hit with a bat or ball and get seriously injured because we didn't have any helmets.

There was one time during a little league game when I was supposed to be wearing a helmet and I wasn't. My friend Nick, one of my high school teammates, was on deck. I walked through the on deck circle but he didn't see me. He swung with a metal bat and hit me in the head. Actually, a wooden or metal bat would have done the same damage. That might have been my first hard hit I got to my head and it looks like I didn't want to stop there. In fact, I didn't!

A few of my good friends from my hometown liked to play baseball but no one had a passion for it like I did. In the summers I always asked my father to bring me to the little league fields down the street and throw me batting practice. He could throw off the little league diamond pretty easily but when it came the time when I moved up to the big diamond he couldn't handle that. I had to find other ways to hit every day.

One day, I was looking through a catalog and saw something that would really help me improve at the plate. It was called a solo hitter and it is the same thing as hitting off a tee but it had a ball on a string so when you hit it, it would come back to where it was. I put it down in my garage and it fit perfectly. From the day I set it up, I was down there every night taking as many swings as I could. Hitting off a tee is boring so I set up my CD player down there so I could listen to music as I hit. My mother didn't like that because I would turn it up so loud and it would be on every night. Moms can be like that.

When I was thirteen, I headed off to Masconomet Regional High School in nearby Boxford, Massachusetts. All I could think about was baseball. Studies were just something I had to do so I could focus on my true passion, baseball. My freshman year started out like most, scary at the beginning, hard at some points and easier at others. It always made me feel good when I would pass some seniors in the hallway and get a hello from them. They knew I played baseball but I had to wait until the spring to show them what I could really do. In the winter I passed the time playing basketball on the freshman team.

Then came spring and baseball started. Coach Delani, the varsity head coach, knew who I was before tryouts started from what he heard about my time playing AAU baseball. During tryouts I threw and hit with the upperclassmen that were already on the team. I was feeling great. I hit the ball hard and fielded the ball smoothly, but then came the running.

I didn't think it would be too bad so I was running as hard as I could for the first few suicides. Then it went to 4 to 5 to 6 and finally ended at 14. Some kids, mostly the freshman, started to take it easy after the 8th or 9th sprint, but I knew I couldn't do that. I had to keep running hard so I would make the team, not junior varsity, but the Varsity Team. I am happy to say that I did make the Varsity Team. I played all through high school and became the team captain in my junior year and again in my senior year. I was on top of the world. I had an abundance of friends, a beautiful girlfriend, and I was the number one baseball player in the state. I was on top of the world and on top of my game. I was recruited by many colleges all down the East Coast but I made the decision to go to Wheaton College in Norton, Massachusetts to play for Coach Podbelski. Looking back with the benefit of hindsight, I can see now that Wheaton was not a good choice for me.

The summer after I graduated high school I felt things were really going my way. I was going to be on my own and finally playing for a college baseball team. Life was good. There were a lot of parties and celebrations. Everyone was eager to start the next phase of their lives. Then there was that one party – the party that forever changed me.

One night changed my views about life, about everyone in my life and everyone in the world. I have the utmost respect for everyone who believed in me and has been there for me since my accident. They never judged me because of the way I talked, things I did and what I can't do as a result of my brain injury. They continue to love and support me unconditionally.

## Chapter Three

## The People Who Define My Life

*"Always turn a negative situation into a positive situation."*

~Michael Jordan

As time passed after my accident, I started to write and think about where I have been throughout my life, where I was and all the different people I have met since 2002. Where I am today is someplace that no one ever thought was possible. I had the world at my fingertips with a bright future ahead of me. After my mistake on August 14, 2002, it was like I was shot out of a cannon. Would I want to change any of it? That is a question on my mind that is unanswered to this day.

If you are down then get up. Work hard and take the negative situation you are in and turn it into a positive. Those who say that attitude is everything understand this better than most people.

All I write is from what I can remember. This gets a bit clearer every day because of the years of brain therapy I have completed, as well as from stories I have been told and told again from my friends and family about things I once couldn't remember. For my first three years after my release from the hospital I couldn't remember what I had for breakfast an hour later. However over the years my memory has improved and continues improving even today. Brain injury recovery is lifelong. I understand and accept this today. As long as I have a heartbeat, my recovery continues.

I have met so many different people since my brain injury that I never thought I would meet or even want to meet. I have met very strong people along my journey who have very serious life challenges who have shown me how lucky I am to be where I am. They all helped me appreciate the life I was given back. I know where I could be right now. I could have been so much worse off. This is part of what drives me. I keep working hard every day because I have a dream! I must get back as close to where I was and to where I was going. If I don't do that I will feel like a quitter and that's just not who I am.

My brain injury gave me a new and unexpected set of challenges. Both my long and short-term memory have been affected. I cannot remember going to high school with any degree of clarity. The worst is that I can't remember my senior year of high school at all. This was my best year on the baseball field. Not remembering many other things that happened in my entire life is very hard for me. But my hardships have strengthened me.

I've had to work very hard to remember the people I have worked with, played with and some who coached me. I could be looking at old photograph of me playing baseball in little league and not recognize who was in the picture. I would have to ask my mother, who the person was in the picture. She would remind me that it is Mr. Dunn, the assistant coach of our little league team. Such was the shattered state of my memories.

In third grade I started little league and I concentrated on playing shortstop because I was the most talented at it. Mr. Dunn and my mother were my little league coaches and they worked together perfectly. When she coached we didn't lose very often. Being the coach's son I don't think had any effect on my playing time. My skill level long after she was my coach showed that. Having my mother as my coach was great because all the other male coaches thought they could roll right over us. Who wants to lose to a girl? But they did and we loved it.

Every year from third to sixth grade she was my coach and at the end of two seasons we walked away with a town championship trophy.

It's a myth that girls can't do anything as good or can't compete with guys. One example that comes to my mind is from the movie, "The Sandlot." When one of the movie characters said to another, "You play ball like a girl." Everything immediately went silent as that is the worst insult anyone can give someone when playing baseball.

The years my mother was my coach changed that stereotype. She sparked the competitive intensity I have. I still use that competitive fire in everything I do. Not only because she did something that was out of the ordinary by coaching a guy's sport in baseball, but because we won when she coached. That is when winning became what I always wanted to do. Nothing can beat having the heart of a champion. My mother took that to another level. She showed that she wasn't afraid of anything by becoming a coach.

The reason baseball became my life and why I love it so much was not because it always came easier to me than other things. Rather, it was because of the people I was surrounded by who made it fun. My parents gave up so much so I would be able to improve as a player and reach my dream. Their encouragement is what kept me going when I didn't want to anymore. It is my mother's belief in me that helps me believe in myself and gives me confidence to keep working hard. To keep doing what I love by pushing me and giving me everything I need along the way. I don't want to know where I would be without her. Because of what she taught me I can't give anything less than 110%. Everyone needs someone in their life to give them an extra push when they need it. I am so happy to have that person be so close to me. She always understood that the game means everything to me.

My mother grew up around the sport with all of her brothers playing. Both of my grandfathers were also very good athletes, so I like to say that baseball is in my blood. By playing for my mother I got used to winning all the time. I went on from there doing the same. That was when my obsession with being the best I can be and being a winner started.

In sports, winning is everything but winning isn't really the joy of the game. Rather, it's working hard and showing you are a winner. The minute I stepped onto a baseball diamond, she began to teach me how to be the best. I pitched some but played shortstop mostly. That was position I grew into and excelled at.

All my life I have been extremely competitive. However, when it came to school and the work that came with it I wasn't as competitive. School came much easier to me until 2004 when I started to take classes again. That was then when I had to really start working harder. The reality was that trying in school was not fun for me so I usually never did try as hard as I could. I was accepted and was on my way to a very good college in 2002 not because I got decent grades. The real reason I was accepted was because of my baseball ability.

I will always work for and play the game I love, but my real challenge after my accident was to get back to socializing with people. That will help me get back to as normal a life as possible, however it will never change the way I am. I live to compete and feel I am back again to win. I now have more confidence in myself because I know I can go through and overcome anything that tries to stop me. There are people in my life who don't believe in me. They only push me and motivate me to work harder and make me want it more. There is inherent power to be found by staying focused on the positive.

Being as competitive as I am, I feel baseball was the perfect sport for me. You need to compete when you play any sport but in baseball, if you don't have a competitive drive you do nothing for the team you play for. Baseball has driven me from day one of my life. Without something like the game to work for, I wouldn't want to do anything. I never enjoyed going to school but I love the game because I live to win and compete.

Competing is something totally different than God-given talent. You can have all the talent in the world but if you come to a field, a court or a rink not ready to compete you might as well just have stayed home. If you don't come to a game ready to win, why play? No one likes to lose.

My competitiveness would sometimes get on peoples nerves but when I was in the hospital, released and home from all my rehab centers doing nothing with my life for years, I saw it for what it really was. My brain injury gave me the biggest challenge of my life and it will take all the strength I have to overcome and beat that challenge. It was a challenge given to me to show what I can really overcome in the face of adversity. I now realize that I can do something meaningful to change the way people look at life. I wanted the game when I was young. I want it now as well so I continue to work hard to get in a position to play at a higher level.

After my brain injury I still wanted to get to Wheaton College, but in the back of my mind I knew it would be a long shot for me to graduate. I was given back to the world to show that with determination, hard work, belief in yourself and a competitive drive you can do anything.

The game is in my blood and is always there to motivate me to do something with it. It is there for me to show that the belief I have in myself and with my determination the possibilities I have in front of me are endless. You have to find something that motivates you and use it to carry you to that place you never thought you could be. That is a lesson I have learned from what I have gone through, the people I have met, watched and even heard about since 2002.

Don't ever give up, fight for what you want and if you work hard enough you can get it. Michael Jordan is an example of that. He didn't give up after he was cut from his high school basketball team and look where his heart, determination and drive got him. Baseball is a game that is not only fun, but that really has been a teacher of life and the driving force to wake up and work hard every day. Everyone needs someone or something in their life so they can enjoy getting up every morning.

I am lucky because I have both, the game and my mother. I have to make her proud for all the sacrifices she made for me after 2002. I do all I can to show that everything she did for me was for something.

She tells me that she is already proud of me, probably for getting through what I have but I need to do something to make her proud of me again. I want her to know for the rest of her life that I didn't give up and made something of myself and she was the biggest part of it. Because of her, I will never give up on my dream. I believe she was put in my life to give me the strength, motivation and the extra push I needed for the biggest challenge of my life.

What everyone should take from a story like mine is inspiration because I show that anything is possible. My life went up, down, side-to-side and all around after I made the biggest mistake of my life. But if others can learn, can be inspired and are offered hope, maybe my mistake can be a blessing to others, a force of true and meaningful motivation.

If you fall you have to get back up and try again because you never know what you can do if you don't get up. It is going just one step farther than you think you can that will give you confidence to achieve what you want. If you have a dream, remember it is your dream. Belief in your self is the first step towards greatness.

You might have to find someone to help you find your purpose in life. I know that I needed help. Luckily I found her close by to help, push and encourage me when I needed it the most. That person is my mother because without her you wouldn't be reading this. I believe she was put in my life to help me get through my biggest challenge. I needed her help more than I ever wanted to ask and she was always there to give it. I hope everybody has someone who they can count on to be there for them when they need it just like I do.

My story is a long one with stories about myself, the people I met on my journey back, everyone who has affected my life, everyone who helped me get to where I am today and the lessons I have learned since 2002. The positive people in my life who stuck to their word and have been there for me still today all helped me get to where I thought I would never be. I am forever grateful for those who stuck by me.

# Chapter Four

## Life in Rehab & Beyond

*"Some people want it to happen, some wish it would happen, and others make it happen."*

~Michael Jordan

In September of 2003 I was sent to Spaulding Rehabilitation Hospital in Boston. Spaulding has the reputation of being one of the best of its kind in rehabilitative medicine in the country. I was still in a coma so I don't remember too much about it, just what I've been told. However, because my memory has improved so I can now remember much more. Most of it might be from the blue notebook that I received when I got home. It was a notebook that my friends would write in everyday when they came to visit me, from beginning to end. I've heard that, "Good friends care for each other, close friends understand each other, but true friends stay forever, beyond words, beyond distance, beyond time." This has been my experience.

As I write you will see some of the quotes that came from that notebook. All of my friends from high school and more came to visit me. Nicole wrote the most, because she was there every day.

*"I have been here every day and night watching you and waiting to see your eyes open. I want to be the first person you see when you wake up to be me. Yesterday I tried going home but I felt like I was leaving you so I came right back". ~Nicole*

The eight floor was the floor at the rehab was for the brain injured patients. It was there that I was taught to speak and walk again. It was funny because all my nurses and therapists, on the floor had similar names –Mia, Lea, La and Tia. They were very attractive blondes so it was easy for me to remember them. The doctors and nurses were all very nice and helped me so much. When I had to shower in the morning, one of the male nurses had to be in the shower with me to make sure I didn't fall. When I think about that, you couldn't pay me enough to watch a man shower but it was what I needed at the time. "Why couldn't one of my hot blonde nurses give me a shower?" I asked myself.

After about a month at Spaulding I began to come out of the coma. I didn't know what happened. I looked up and saw my family and friends around the bed. I couldn't walk or talk much. Then soon after, I blew my mother a kiss goodbye. Everyone cried with happiness. Nicole and her parents came to see me every day. My bed was netted so I couldn't get out if someone was not in the room. Some of my friends and family would jump in and lie with me at night. The hospital room had a big reclining chair for the visitors but it wasn't very comfortable. They made my Dad sleep there and being 6 foot 6, it could not have been too comfortable. As a parent he felt it was his job to be there and take care of me.

My parents didn't want me to be there alone during the day and at night because I had no way of using the buzzer to call a nurse if I got myself in trouble. They made a schedule for my friends and family to come and stay with me. I'm not sure what the other patients did without the support system I had. My high school baseball coach, Peter Delani (Coach D), would come and spend every Thursday night with me. I don't know how he did it because he had work and family to go to the next day. One day he put a baseball in my hand and asked me to hold a split finger fast ball. After a few tries I did it. He was so excited he called my mother immediately to give her the good news. One little step forward for me was a huge deal.

All coaches are there for their players when they play for them but Coach D went well beyond that. He is someone I know I will be able to count on for the rest of my life. He gave me a chance to play for him when I was a small, skinny fourteen-year-old freshman and has helped me ever since. Our relationship started out like all player/coach relationships but the relationship we have now has turned into something much more than that.

I took his philosophy class during my junior year of high school and it was the best class I ever took in high school. He had us read books I never would have read if I didn't take his class. He would have us read 400 page books that were more interesting and fun to read than anything else. We read books that really made us think about life. Books like, *Tuesday's with Morrie,* a book about an old man who is dying and knew he was dying but kept on loving his life because he knew he affected so many others.

I learned about the reality of people who are in real bad shape and continue to live there life as well as they can. Being in his class and the books I read it taught me how to overcome challenges. What I learned from him both on and off the field helped me get through the four years before I made it to Wheaton College. He not only taught me about the game I love but taught me how to win and about life at the same time.

When people around me talked about school I always brought up his class and said it was the only class that the books he had us read I read cover-to-cover. They were much more interesting than any English book I was given because the books taught you about life.

I was real close with Coach D throughout my high school days because I played on his team and was the biggest star on the team. He did a lot for me then but he did the most for me after I graduated high school, at a time that he had no obligation to. He is a professional scout for the Colorado Rockies and was in Chicago at a meeting the night of my crash. He got the call on August 14, 2002 and told that I was in a coma and that no one what was going to happen. At that time I already graduated high school so you would think our relationship would be over. Not so for Coach Delani. He got on the first flight back to Boston to see me the minute he heard about it.

I helped him coach his team in 2004 when I was home. I became friendly with a few of his players. It was good to have them around because most of the kids I graduated with who were around were no longer friends. They treated me like a real person and not a nothing like some others thought I became. There was a freshman when I was a senior who became my best friend on the team. Allen didn't care about my brain injury and liked me for me, not just for who I was to everyone else. We would train together and hang out all the time, like friends do.

Allen went to school in Florida and invited me down to see him. It was a great trip until the last couple of days. We were out pretty late and hadn't gotten much sleep that week. I got up in the middle of the night to use the bathroom. I have a tendency to sleep walk when I am in unfamiliar places. I fell asleep and landed in between the wall and the toilet. The light from the bathroom woke Allen up and he yelled, "What are you doing?!" I said, "I don't know, I fell and I can't get up."

I crawled back to bed and woke up the next morning with two front teeth missing. I thought I was dreaming at first so I thought if I went back to sleep they would be there when I woke up. And you know what? They still weren't there. Luckily it was my last night there. We went to the beach that day and I got completely sunburned and my face started to blister. Allen's mother put some bandages on my burns to help them heal. Then I was off to the airport. I totally forgot that I had these bandages on my face. When I met my mother at the airport she almost fainted when she saw me. She told me to go look in the mirror and when I did I started laughing at myself. Those poor people on the plane who saw me must have been pretty scared!

I also took Allen on a family vacation in 2007 to Costa Rica. My sister brought her friend and my brother brought his wife. Bringing Allen was a good choice because he kept us laughing. We went to a bar and for some reason he felt he should pick up a chair, carry it above his head and walk around the room with it yelling "I am king of this island". Now who does that? Some things you just don't forget. Learning to laugh again after a brain injury is healing.

I went into my high school in 2006 to talk to Coach D and I asked him if he was still teaching. He said he wasn't and laughed at my question, thinking the only reason I liked his class was because of all the good looking senior girls in the class. I laughed with him but that was definitely not the reason.

My brain injury taught me how far I can go if I was at the bottom and how to look deep inside myself to find the extra strength I needed to keep going. I am lucky that Coach D taught me that and I remembered it. That lesson is something I needed and what I have used every day since I was back on my feet. I will be using the lessons I learned from him for the rest of my life.

Let's circle back to my time at Spaulding Rehab. My mother's best friend, Lisa, came in to see me all the time. One day she came in with a signed baseball by Pedro Martinez, a former Boston Red Sox Hall of Fame pitcher. I was outside my room and she was down the hall with the ball. She told me that if I could wheel myself over to her then she would give me the ball. So, I became determined to do it.

I have always been up for a challenge. I started wheeling myself over to her, really slow because the muscles in my arms wouldn't let me go any faster. I finally made it to her and it was like I won the World Series. Everyone there was so excited that I did it and I was excited because I won a signed baseball by one of the best pitchers in baseball history. I still have that ball in my bedroom and every time I see it I think of that amazing day. But that was just the start of me coming back. I said to myself then, "I should have got up and walked to her, and then I really would of surprised people."

I was in a wheelchair because my legs were so weak from being in the same position for 60 days and I had also lost 60 pounds. If I did try to walk I would have taken one step and fallen right on my face. After a while I was able to cruise around in my wheel chair pretty well. But they always tied me in it so I wouldn't fall out. One day my dad was wheeling me around and stopped to talk to someone. He let the wheelchair go and I went slamming into a door. Everyone came rushing over to help. I think my Dad was still talking.

The Spaulding stories continue. One afternoon my mother couldn't find me. After getting everyone on the floor to search, she found me in my roommate's bed. I somehow slipped down through the ropes that were holding me in my wheel chair, got up and climbed into his bed – luckily he wasn't there. Then there was the Halloween party at Spaulding hospital and all the nurses dressed me up. They put a Hawaiian T shirt on me and decorated my wheel chair. I only know this from pictures of myself I have seen. In the picture I was smiling like I was a 6 year old about to go out trick or treating. Finally I was discharged from Spaulding and allowed to go home. But I didn't get to go home. I was shipped off to another facility where more unexpected challenges awaited me.

## Chapter Five

## The Middleboro Shuffle

*"Limits, like fears, are often illusions."*

~ Michael Jordan

In December of 2002 I was moved to The Greenery in Middleboro, Massachusetts. The Greenery was a rehabilitation center for people with brain injuries and other disabilities. I was there for six long weeks. The team at Spaulding recommended it to my parents so I didn't have much of a choice.

When I got to Middleboro and saw the patients there I knew I was in for a long and hard haul. I was not overly fond of being there. The rooms were filled with people with all sorts of problems – people with brain injuries, people whose entire bodies were so damaged that they couldn't walk, talk or live on their own and people with mental challenges or drug addictions that destroyed their brains. The most upsetting was all the people in the hallways who were placed in wheelchairs and just left there. No one came to visit them. They were left like they were not important. Although now I don't really remember being there, I do get pictures in my head about what it looks like and how hard it was for me being there. I'm hoping those mental pictures stop coming because I hate to even think about it.

I did come home for holidays and sometimes on weekends. Middleboro didn't like it when patients would leave for a weekend and threatened to give beds away if they did. That was something no one could understand. Why would they be against being with family and people who loved you for a faster recovery?

Daily I met up with therapists and was given a notebook to write about my days, every day, hour-by-hour. However, because my memory was so bad I would constantly lose my notebook. Thankfully another one of the patients, Ray, would find it and return it to my dad for me. He was so proud of himself. When Ray would see my father he would say "Mr. Bransfield, I found Tim's book again yesterday, you should tell him to hold on to it". I'm not sure what happened to Ray but I was told that no one ever came to visit him. That is just sad.

I was supposed to read the book later so it would spark my memory. I'm not sure if it really helped because at that time I couldn't even remember the book, much less what was in it. As matter of fact, I used to call my mother fifty or more times a day, because I wouldn't remember calling in the first place. The nurses wanted to take my phone away but my mother fought that because it was the only thing I had. She had a lot of patience, but I'm not sure her coworkers did − hearing the phone ringing all day long!

My roommate at the Greenery was an older man who was there because his brain had deteriorated from too much alcohol and drugs. He would always tell me stories about his life and how he ended up there and how much fun he used to have with the different types of drugs he took. I would ask myself,

"Why is he telling me this, who does he think I am?" But he did have something wrong with his brain. My mother told me once that he was going out with his ex-wife for the day and he laid out about twelve pairs of jeans on his bed. He just couldn't decide which pair to wear. He would try them on, then take them off and try again. This is what a brain injury can do to you. As tough as my journey can be, it could have been so much worse.

My father would drive down every morning to take me out to breakfast. When he arrived and walked in the front door, May, another patient, was always there to give him hugs and kisses. For some reason she was always eating crackers and had crackers stuck in her teeth. So when she would come close to hug him she would spit crackers in his face. It always made me laugh.

Middleboro was not my favorite place and I am so lucky I was only there for six weeks. I was lucky to there in the first place, but the time I spent there showed me how really lucky I am. I know from living there how much worse it could have been for me.

When I was at Spaulding I met Ronnie. Ronnie had just graduated from college when he was the passenger in the car of a drunk driver. He was a kid just like me, in a car accident like mine and is now in a wheel chair, maybe for the rest of his life. You know what the worst thing about it is? The driver of that car walked away fine and he never came to visit Ronnie. The most likely reason that he never comes to see him must be that he feels bad and doesn't want to see what he did to his friend. Such is the power of guilt and shame.

Ronnie and I both ended up at the Middleboro Greenery and the sad thing is that he was there for a total of twelve years until they closed the facility down. For now he is living in the same type of facility in Plymouth, Massachusetts. When I think I have it bad all I have to do is think of him and it shows me how lucky I really am. Life perspectives come in unexpected places. To still be able to walk, talk, have a chance to go to college, have a chance to live a normal life and still be able to play the game I love is a miracle – these make me grateful for what I can still do.

Ronnie is still in a wheelchair and I think sometimes if I was that way, I don't know if I would want to keep living. Ronnie, however, lives every day loving his life. His "never quit" attitude and courage motivates me and anyone who knows him. He works as hard as he can and he is always laughing, smiling and cracking jokes.

I asked my mother all the time, "How is Ronnie doing? Is he still in Middleboro?" "When is he getting out?" The answers are always the same. "Yes, he is still in Middleboro and I don't know if he will ever get out". I think about Ronnie every day and pray that one day he will have a chance to live a free life. If anyone deserves it, he does. Every night I pray for Ronnie and ask to help him with what he is going through and wish him the best. Then one day in 2007 my mother said to me, "Tim, Ronnie is going to be released from Middleboro!"

They were going to get a place set up for him to live in Boston and have people there to help him with everything he needs. I was so excited for him when I heard that news but it never worked out. Something the State couldn't follow through on. It was very disappointing for Ronnie and his family. Ronnie is a very strong and positive person who is in such a bad situation and continues to work hard every day to get his life as good as it can be. Ronnie is someone I will remember and look up to for the rest of my life. I admire him for the courage and strength he displays every day. Real heroes come in many forms. Ronnie was my hero.

I now understand that I was saved by God and that is something I now believe. When I left the Greenery I began to think that if I was saved by God, why wouldn't He help the other people there? If God saved me, why wouldn't He save them? Some things I most likely will never understand.

# Chapter Six

## Learning from Michael Jordon

*"Limits, like fear, are often illusions."*

~Michael Jordan

Looking back with the benefit of a bit of hindsight, in 2002 I had a very exciting future ahead of me. I was planning to attend Wheaton College to be their starting shortstop. However, when I woke up from my coma everything had changed. Many of my closest friends of mine treated me differently. They stopped visiting me and very rarely did any of them invite me to go out with them. The ones who did visit often felt very uncomfortable around me. It was apparent and I could feel it.

It was hard enough to wake up from my coma and deal with the things I went through as part of my ongoing rehabilitation. The reality of it was that their reactions only made things more difficult for me. I never expected that.

During that time I became very depressed, angry, sad and confused. I felt like I was stuck at home relearning everything. Harder still, there were many days when I felt suicidal and I often shared these feelings with others. I wanted this life to end. I regret thinking that way and saying those things about how I felt. I now know that I was at my lowest point. When my mother and I were driving somewhere, I would unbuckle my seatbelt, open the door a little and say, "Mom, this is it, I'm going to do what should have happened years ago."

I understand now how selfish and stupid it was for me to say those kinds of things to her. I didn't care how it happened, I was ready to end my life by just falling out into traffic.

It took me many years to realize I was given the gift of a second chance at life as well as to play the game I love. I feel blessed that I have been able to come as far as I have. There are many who will never have a chance to get to where I am today or a chance to do anything ever again. This perspective could only happen with the passage of time.

From what I have been through and since overcome since 2002, whatever steps in my path to try to stop me, I will beat. The confidence I have in myself helps me keep going. To compete and to win is what I live for because winners are always remembered. If you lose you are easily forgotten and I don't think anyone wants to go to their grave forgotten.

Everyone has someone they look up to. When I first saw the Chicago Bulls play, I was struck by how powerful an athlete Michael Jordan was and I wanted to be like him. I had the passion for the game of baseball just like he had the passion for the game of basketball. He taught me early on in my life how to compete and how to win. When I was growing up I was impressed with him because of the basketball player he was and all the awards he won. I enjoyed watching him play because of the type of competitor he was.

When he quit the Chicago Bulls in the early 90's to play baseball, many though he was just crazy.

Transitions like this simply did not happen in major league sports. Why is he trying baseball when he is already the best in the world at what he does already? Everyone thought he was just making a mockery of the game and was an embarrassment to the game of baseball when he quit basketball. In a video on Michael Jordan I watched frequently, a baseball coach of his said, "If anyone is an embarrassment, I hope they can embarrass me like that."

He left basketball the first time after winning his third world championship and was the best in the world. In his video he explained why he left basketball. He said he always loved baseball, he grew up playing, loved being around the game and it was something his father always wanted him to try to do. So after his third world championship he said, "No one can give me a challenge anymore on the basketball court except for the challenge my father presented to me which was to try and play baseball."

Playing baseball was something no one thought he could do. He was sent to a Chicago White Sox farm team and if he was just a regular guy trying out for the team he probably would have been sent home the first day. But this was Michael Jordan. He was biggest name in all of professional sports. Why wouldn't anyone want him to play for their team?

It is Michael Jordan's devotion to his game that pushes me for the game I love. Throughout my entire life Michael Jordan has been the athlete I wanted to be like, an athlete who, in my own eyes, had no flaws. I admire him because he plays to WIN and with his work ethic and competitiveness when he plays, he WINS.

He started out not doing as well as he had hoped, but "Right before I left baseball I was finding my swing and feeling more comfortable on the field every day."

However even being Michael Jordan could only take him so far. After two years he decided to return to the Chicago Bulls because baseball wasn't working out. He returned to the Bulls. The NBA had a whole new look, with all new faces and star players to go with it. He took it as just another challenge. I have learned so much from Michael Jordan. When I was young and even today, he continues to inspire me.

Most importantly, he taught me how to work hard and to never give up. If someone presents a challenge to you, you can't sit back and do nothing. You have to fight to overcome and get past what others think you can't do.

I took my situation as nothing more than a challenge. No one thought I was able to do anything anymore, ANYTHING. I know today that I didn't wake up for nothing. I'm not back in the world to work at a local gas station like everyone thought Michael Jordan would do when he decided to go to the University of North Carolina.

"Everyone thought I would go to North Carolina for a year, sit on the bench and then come home and work at a local gas station or something," he shared at one point.

Starting in 2003 Michael Jordan gave me determination and confidence to get up every day. Michael Jordan even said, "There will be someone greater than me, they will learn from my example just like I have learned from others."

Even though it was hard, he went to college as nobody and people told him he would be a nobody, and you know what he said to that negativity.

"That is why I will succeed."

Michael Jordan had the most confidence in himself and I have the most confidence in myself because of the challenges I have been faced with and overcome since my brain injury. You need confidence in yourself to succeed. I know I can do anything I put my mind to. That is confidence in yourself and that is how everyone has to live.

Your mind plays a much bigger role to get what you want and that is the mindset I needed and what everyone needs. All the negativity that was around me, towards me and everyone who put me down obviously knows nothing about where I came from and nothing about the person I am. How hard it was for me to get where I am today and how hard I work to get where I want to be. That is why I will succeed. I chose to succeed because of my challenges, not in spite of them.

People close to me and people I have met might think they know but don't if they think that I will fail. I will not. People overcome obstacles every day. Life can be hard. With a strong heart and determination there is always a way. Michael Jordan found a way and I am following his example.

I work hard every day so that when I get my chance I will show what I can still do. I know I will and there is nothing, anyone can say to me that will make me stop. I've come so far and worked too hard to ever give up. I will succeed, I will win. Every athlete needs a mindset like that because without it you will fail but with it you can succeed. I am living proof.

I now realize that I am back in the world to change how people look at what they can do in the face of adversity. To show that with belief in yourself, hard work, dedication and determination to get what you want, anything is possible. My life is a living example of this. I know in my heart that I am doing a good job of that. Not many people ever thought that I would wake up, but I did. No one thought I would walk again but I did that too. No one thought I would make it to a good school like Wheaton College and I got there.

Absolutely no one believed I would be able to play baseball but I knew I could. I made the team at Wheaton College.

I have learned to believe in myself. Now, I'm not saying it was easy, because it wasn't and even today still isn't. I had days when I didn't even want to get up to try. But I would think back to the Michael Jordan's philosophy so I did get up and I'm still getting up today. A successful life, in the face of seemingly overwhelming adversity is not about how often you fall. Rather, it's about picking yourself up and moving forward.

During the first few years that I was home from the hospital people would ask me if I was still playing baseball. Then they would say to me, "You can't do that anymore." When I heard that, the first thought that came to my mind and the first words that came out of my mouth were, "Is that a challenge?" I learned from Michael Jordan to never give up on anything. Live for and work to the limit to win and overcome any challenge I encounter in my life has become my philosophy. People face challenges every day, some small, some big. I was faced with a challenge in 2002 and I feel I am succeeding and I will win because of the positive people I have in my life, people who really believe in me.

Some people don't have it in them so they don't even try but if you want something bad enough then you have to find a way.

Now a challenge takes on a whole new meaning to me. Previously I won because my skills took over. When I woke up from my coma, my skills weren't close to what they were so I took it as only an ordeal I had to overcome. That is why I continued to hit every day and continued to work to play shortstop because no one thought I could.

When I got to Wheaton College in the fall of 2006, reality set in. I was a top recruit in 2002 so the coach knew about my brain injury. He knew I probably wouldn't be able to play shortstop or any in field position anymore because my athletic ability wouldn't be what it was when he was recruiting me, or maybe not good enough to play at all.

Then he saw me throwing at practice, put me on the mound and made me a pitcher right away. I took it as just another test of my endurance. What better than to start off my college career than with a challenge? Not only was I going to Wheaton College but I was back on the baseball diamond. These were two things no one thought I would ever be able to do. When I was back on my feet in 2003 those were the two things I had to do. I made them believe that every swing I took was going to be a game winner. You really can cover a lot of ground with a good attitude. My own life shows this.

## Chapter Seven

## Rebuilding a Life Continues

*"If you accept the expectations of others, especially negative ones, then you never will change the outcome."*

~Michael Jordan

When I came home in February of 2003 I still needed a lot of help, more help than I initially was willing to admit. My hard work and progress were going well, but I still had such a long way to go. I felt like I was literally trapped in Topsfield for three years after my brain injury. Even worse, I thought I would be stuck there for the rest of my life. Without a car and with no one around, life was very hard for me and depression set in. The last three years living in Topsfield, every day was about same. I woke up and when I didn't have any therapy to go to I would walk down the street with our dog Mugsy to give him some exercise and have breakfast at the Day Break Café. I always liked to eat out because I thought food at a restaurant was better than food at home no matter where it was. Paying for a burger or any food meant that it was a better meal, even if it wasn't. I also liked getting out of the house and seeing people.

A brain injury can be so isolating. This daily contact with people helped me to not be so isolated. Every morning my mother would leave some money on the counter before she went to work so I could do that. I guess that is what mothers are for; to know everything about their kids. I have the best mother of all.

Before 2003 I don't think I ever went to the Day Break Café, but when I came home, Billy, the owner, threw me a party. It was a surprise and it seemed like everyone I knew came. It made me feel really good. I am grateful to Billy for his kindness.

It was three years after my hospital stay when I intentionally tried to forget all the people who said they would always be there and weren't. During my first three years home I would call them every day, usually a few times a day. Some a few times in the same hour because I forgot I called. My bad memory got on many people's nerves, mine as well. One friend told me that I changed and I am not the same person I used to be so that was why he stopped wanting to be around me. I now understand this this is very common among brain injury survivors. Survivors lose friends. Some studies show that up to 80% of close friends choose to walk away within the first year after a brain injury. While I never counted, I did indeed have many, many friends choose to not be part of my life anymore.

The reality is that a near death experience will change anyone. It has changed my views on life after seeing and meeting the people I had met after 2002. I have learned to love life and every second of it. I began to believe the reason I had a lot of friends in high school was only because of my athletic reputation. That is why I would definitely change the crowd I hung around with.

If I could go back in time, I would also change the style of my game. From little league through high school I trained to be dominant at the plate. I worked so hard that I felt I could do what I wanted to at the plate and in fact, I did at that time. It is too bad that I have no meaningful memory of when I was the best player and hitter in the state. Everything that happened during my junior year in high school I thought for years happened in my senior year. I now know that I was a full year off. My brain therapist told me that more memories will come back as my brain continues to heal.

I do remember my mother telling me after I was released from the hospital that it would take six to nine years for me to be as close to 100% both mentally and physically as I could be. That was what the doctors told her, I thought. She told me six years later that they never gave her a specific number. So I don't know if she said that to me just to make me feel good because when she told me the doctors didn't know, it only made me feel worse.

Then there was my dog Mugsy. I know what you are thinking. Why is Tim talking about his dog? But Mugsy was with me from day one, every second of every day. Obviously he didn't have a choice and didn't really know how I felt about him, being an animal. But animals have an intuitive sense and I really think he did know. When my mother decided to put him down in 2008 it was like I lost my best friend. I would say that my mother did it to him because I was totally against it. Why would someone want to do that to their best friend? On the other hand he was very old and was suffering. He was fourteen years old and our veterinarian told us that he had a brain disease. He started going to the bathroom in the house, staring at walls for long periods of time and really didn't know where he was. If he was human, she would have sent him the Middleboro Greenery for some brain therapy. After a long time my mother convinced me that we had to put him down. She told me he wasn't having fun living anymore. The day we put him down was hard. He was there for me when it really mattered and when I needed him the most.

He was there when I went to bed and slept right next to me, there to watch me leave for CRC in 2003 and always waiting for me at the front door when I got home. When I got home my mother would call the house and say, "Tim can you take the dog out?" So I did, but I didn't walk him. I just opened the front door to let him run where he wanted. However, Mugsy wasn't much of a runner.

He was a pug and every day he wandered into the center of town to get food from the stores and restaurants. Everyone knew who he was because he was so friendly and always around. For being so small he was not small in belly region. Free food will do that to a dog, you know. He would sit outside the stores in town waiting to get food and more often than not he did. I would get a call from an owner of a store in town saying, "We have your dog down here, and do you want to come get your dog so he doesn't get hit by a car?"

He always made it home alright so I would tell them just to let him go, he will be fine. Then an hour later he made his way back to our front door.

I remember one time when my mother and I were both outside calling for him. A few minutes later we saw him running down the street. He was far away but as he got closer my mother and I said to each other, "What is that in his mouth?"

He made it back to the driveway and we saw he traveled from the center of town with a giant bagel in his mouth. That was Mugsy for you. He loved to eat and did it well, all the time. Companionship was critical to my recovery. It didn't matter if it was two-legged of four-legged. I couldn't have asked for any better dog.

When I was released from the hospital at the end of 2002 my girlfriend Nicole, her family and my entire family were there for me. When I went to the Middleboro Greenery my parents and Nicole came to visit me every week. Most of my good friends were in college by this time, but Nicole took an entire year off from school to help me the first year I was home in 2003. That first year my memory was so bad I once couldn't remember a thing from it. The brain therapy I have done has brought back some memories of the early years after 2003 as well as memories from years before. However some of those days remain forgotten and might be forgotten forever. It is just a price I have to pay for the decision I made the night of my accident.

It wasn't long after I got home that I started a day therapy at Community Rehab Care (CRC) in Medford, Massachusetts. Every morning for eight months I went from 9:00 AM to 2:00 PM. The rehab was only 20 minutes away from my house. I say only because it was the longest 20 minute drive I've ever taken. The patients there were the total opposite of the ones I met at the Middleboro Greenery.

As I was there I always wondered why I was there. I'd ask myself, "Why am I here? Is it just for torture?" Every day I was at CRC working to get my mind and my life back.

I was there and all the while hating myself and hating my life and all I wanted to do was sleep. I didn't understand my brain injury and couldn't understand why I was had to go to CRC and why I had to be picked up by "The Ride". The Ride is a service provided by the State of Massachusetts to drive people who can't get to their therapies, doctor appointments or wherever they need to go. I didn't like the fact that "The Ride" was in big letters on the side of the door and everyone knew there was something wrong with the passengers inside. I felt different.

My mother was at work in the morning before I got up so sometimes when I wasn't moving at all. My Dad would often come down and try to get me up. He would take my dog Mugsy, in one hand and toss him like a football at me. After almost an hour of fighting with me, he would call my mother and have her talk to me. "Tim, this is your last day, just go today and you are done." So I was on my way and you know what? Six months later I was still there. You would think I would be mad and I was at the time, but I see now that it was the best thing for me. I still had a great desire to get my old life back and this was the only way to do it. One little step at a time.

Some days, "The Ride" would be outside honking and I would still be in bed. But then I would hear, "Oh Tim, time to get up, we have CRC today!" I would pretend that I was sleeping so Sally would go away. Sally also had a brain injury but was a funny lady who loved going to CRC. Sally was considered the class clown of the group. I knew I didn't have a chance of staying home when Sally came by. I can still hear her voice!

"Tim, time to wake up we have CRC today."

The first few weeks I would get dropped off at the front door of CRC. I would say to myself, "What do I do now?" I didn't even know where to go. After of few days of continually being late to therapy class they would have someone waiting for me to show me the way. Eventually, I was able to make it on my own.

All of the therapists and patients at CRC made my time there enjoyable no matter how much I didn't want to be there. Some were my age while many were much older, but they were in similar shape as me. Although we had different injuries, we had a lot in common. I don't know why they were there but I knew it must have been something bad. I never asked them and they never asked me.

The one person I remember the most was Amy. She was the director of the group. I don't know how she did it but she made us all feel good. I can still remember all of the patients: Jim, Rob, Tiffany, Bill, Dominique and of course Sally. Rob loved rap music and we would constantly argue about who was the best. Jim was from the same town as a friend of mine from AAU baseball so I would tell him that, probably a few too many times. But I don't think he noticed. You see, when you have a brain injury like mine you tend to repeat yourself a lot because you don't remember saying it the first time. They probably repeated themselves too, but then it was okay because most likely I didn't remember it the first time.

I was the last of the group to leave CRC in September of 2003. I was ready to leave. I often think of my friends there and wonder what they are doing now but I don't have any way to find them. CRC helped me socially more than anything. The strange thing about my brain injury is that I couldn't remember much when I was there but now I do remember it. Such are the memory challenges of living with a brain injury. I am grateful for the experience and the companionship I had with so many others who shared my fate.

## Chapter Eight

Training to Live, Living to Train

*"I can accept failure, everyone fails at something,
but I can't accept not trying."*

~Michael Jordan

My physical therapy at CRC wasn't proving to be enough for me so I had to go to the gym and begin training on my own. I worked out virtually every day to play shortstop and I started working with a personal trainer. "Rep" was my personal trainer the summer before I went to Wheaton College in 2006.

"Rep," was the best personal trainer I have ever had the chance to work with. In 2005, I was in my gym and I saw his promotional poster on the wall. On his poster were a number of professional athletes. Suffice to say, his resume and credentials looked good. I started working with him on a one-on-one basis. He helped me find the exercises I needed to do to be the best shortstop I could be. Under his guidance, I became stronger and more confident every day. This dramatically enhanced my ability on the baseball field.

We first started working on my upper body strength so I could hit the ball hard and far. I was trying to get back to the performance level I had achieved before my brain injury. Every day I got stronger and thank "Rep" for the push he gave me. I always have the motivation to do the type of physical work required because it is in my heart to work hard. He gave me the extra push I sorely needed.

He also trained other athletes as well. One day, while in the gym, I was playing a basketball pickup game with one of his trainees, Katie. We played for a little while, each of us making a few baskets. In two ticks of a clock, I found myself on the ground. Playing her, I rolled my ankle, limped painfully and humbly off the court.

I needed to go to the doctor to get it x-rayed to see if I had broken my ankle. The doctor came in with the X-rays. My folder of X-rays was big enough for an entire town. The doctor let me know that my ankle was broken and casted it. The next day I went to the gym on my crutches and saw Rep and the two girls I was playing against the day before. Rep smiled and laugh a bit and said, "You broke your ankle playing a girl." To this day I have not played basketball against anyone. The only time I play is when I shoot around by myself. I am not taking a chance on breaking any more bones.

On August 14, 2002, the date my accident occurred, I broke over 15 bones at one time along with other injuries to my body. These days, I choose to stick to strictly lifting weights for baseball and playing baseball, nothing more. It's just safer for me.

In my hometown of Lynn, Massachusetts everyone knew my grandfather by his nickname. Townspeople fondly called my grandfather "Bumps." It is a nickname that he earned from all the different injuries he had throughout his long life. When I was in my coma, one of my frequent visitors penned a note in the blue book  that my visitors used to write me notes. She wrote: "Your dad and I were talking. As the name Bumps was already taken, we decided your new nickname is Crash.

That name fit me well. I can't change what happened so I guess I deserved the name. From here, however, to the end of my life I will try not to do anything that will break another bone. I realized though that all my broken bones as well as my time in a coma only made me tougher and stronger both mentally and physically. I am much stronger for having gone through all this.

In my life I feel have been given many advantages. I have experienced and also overcome so many things and done things people said couldn't be done. I have come back from all sorts of injuries. I suffered had many broken bones, three concussions as well as a three month coma. I have been accident prone my entire life but I always get through life throws at me. I always come back stronger than I was before. My brain injury is not any different. Nothing could match the pain I have gone through, mentally and physically since August 14, 2002. I went into a coma and woke up on a mission. I continue to climb the ladder to get back everything I lost to be more then prepared when I get my chance on the baseball diamond.

During this time, I learned many lessons. I learned that having a personal trainer can help you become stronger. A personal trainer that can help you become stronger, faster and more confident in your athletic ability is another lesson learned. That is exactly what Rep did for me that summer. I felt more confident in my abilities by the time I arrived at Wheaton College because I saw how much I improved every day. Having a trainer who has worked with some of the best athletes in the world is not a bad one to have also. If you are going to take the time to train, why settle for less?

I couldn't wait to get to Wheaton College to show the results of my hard work. I was down for so long. Soon it would be my time again. I would make all the people who have helped me since 2002 so happy and proud because I have come so far because of what they did for me. I wanted to prove that I still had the ability to play short stop and the skills to hit just like I used to. But I secretly held the belief that I do it even better because I worked so hard at it. The negative people in my life made me want it more and the positive people who believed in me motivated me to work harder.  People like my mother, my home town friends, Jackie and Don and so many more.

I got to know many of Reps other clients as well. One of his clients Jess was my favorite. She soon my best friend at the gym.  The kids I worked out with that summer while training with Rep were all very nice and didn't treat me any different than anyone else. None of them were baseball players. Some were only in high school and were mostly basketball or soccer athletes. I loved working with all of them because I always felt comfortable being around them. They never judged me and I felt none of them thought that they were better than me. It was a wonderful time in my recovery.

The first couple years I worked with Rep, he would give me a hard time about some of the things I said. But at that time, I never thought about what I going to say before I said it. It must have been pretty annoying to those close to me. After a few years, he started giving me compliments on how much I improved since the first day I met him. His compliments always made me feel good.  I still improve physically every day and

I work very hard to improve my brain everyday so that too will improve my game.

After a while of working with Rep he told me to slow it down. Always one to push myself harder, I still did much more than I should have. During the early years that I was working with him I could be pretty bothersome as I was pretty obsessed with getting ready for Wheaton College. I would call him every night with a question about what I should do the next day, sometimes the same question. I remember calling him one night. He answered the phone with a raspy voice and said, "Tim what do you want? I have to wake up in 7 hours to train." Looking back, I see now that I was quite a challenge for Rep.

Most people expected me to quit trying in 2003. But by now, you know that I refuse to quit. I know now that I am not just working for myself. I am working for my mother who always believes in me and has helped me more than anyone from day one. I work hard for my entire family and all of my friends, who helped me, believed in me and supported me, to show that if you work hard to get what you want then you can do anything. You must have the determination and dedication to do the work. My heart and motivation is always there. Motivation is what you need the most. My father tells me I have a heart like a locomotive. I don't argue.

# Chapter Nine

## A Family Affair

*"Always turn a negative situation into a positive situation."*

~Michael Jordan

You would have thought I could have some time to myself when I got home from CRC, but I was not so lucky. My parents were still concerned about me being alone so they put an ad in the paper to find someone to help out. The succeeded - they found Annibal. He was a neurologist from Brazil and they thought that he was a perfect match. Suffice to say, he wasn't. He came to my house two or three times a week. He didn't understand the complexity of life after a brain injury and would spend most of his time just reading and writing in some notebook. He would often read me a story and after every sentence he wrote a three page paper on it. I would go into my room and tell him I was tired and pretend to be asleep. It wasn't because I didn't like the guy and he never made me mad for what he was doing because he was getting paid to do it. Though he tried his best, what he was trying to have me do was far too much for me to handle at that time. I wasn't able to keep up with him because all of his writing didn't make any sense to me. Suffice to say, he didn't last too long.

During this time, I would get home from CRC around 2:00 PM and just sit in front of my computer and wait for my sister to get home from school to take me to the gym. My sister Michaella was my only transportation during the early years that I was at home. The police had taken my license away for three years. This was just another consequence of the mistake I had made. After school my sister would hurry home to check on me and take me to the gym or would sometimes ask her friend, Sara, to do it.

I know Michaella got angry that she had to rush home every day, though I was quite happy she did. This allowed me to get out of the house. I didn't want to ruin her day by being a burden but the reality was that I couldn't help it. I needed to work out so I could play baseball again and I needed to work out so that I could continue to recover. Michaella and I would still fight about little things like most brother and sisters do. I was in a hole and needed her help. Thankfully, she understood.

Michaella began to hang out with many of the friends I had from high school. She already knew quite a few of them from when they came to visit me in the hospital. I would hear stories about her from my friends when I talked to them and stories from her about those same kids. I would ask myself why she was hanging out with them. But more importantly, I wondered why they were not hanging out with me. It made me angry at first that some of my good friends were with my little sister and not me anymore. Over time, I began to realize that I was not the same person I used to be. My personality had changed. I worked hard every day to come back a better person but I wasn't there yet.

My brother Bob was already in college. Bob had started his sophomore year was when my accident occurred. He always came to see me because both his college and the hospital I was in were both in Boston. He would also come to our house in Topsfield occasionally. During the school year, Bob wasn't around except for holidays, but during the summers he did all he could do for me, just like the rest of my family. I have learned not to concentrate on what you're siblings don't do but what they do for you. After all, that is what a real family is for.

They did so much for me, more than I would ever ask of them but sometimes they got on my nerves just like I would get on their nerves. Michaella was the only girl in my family and it seemed to me that she got everything she wanted whenever she wanted it. I was not happy about this and she knew it. I believe I felt that way only because her life was going smoothly and well. At this point in time, my life wasn't. Two years after my hospital stay she would rub in my face about everything she did for me. I never liked that because I couldn't do anything about it. I was at the lowest part of my life with a bad memory and needed her help. I hope she knows I feel this way about her now and I hope she understands where I was and how hard it was for me. Looking back, I see that we all did the best we could in the face of very tough circumstances.

My brother paid the price as well. I would often intentionally tease him about things that I knew made him angry. The truth is that I really didn't mean it. I was mad that they both were doing something with their lives while I thought that I would be stuck living with my mother for the rest of mine. They both equally did more than they had to for me and I will never be able to repay them.

I am so happy they didn't put me aside and give up on me like they could have. It took me years to realize that and years more to get back to new and improved better Tim. They understood and for that, I am grateful. If anyone was in my position, I hope they can say that they have brothers and sisters who they can count on like I do. I hope they know that I would do the same for them. Well... maybe, if I remembered.

# Chapter Ten

## Dr. Diane

*"Limits, like fear, is often an illusion."*

~Michael Jordan

By now you would think I would have had quite enough of therapy. The harsh reality was that I was still a long way from getting my life back and my short term memory was still quite bad. I became quite depressed with nothing to do but hang out at home with my dog, Mugsy. My mother understood better than most that I wasn't happy so she gave a call to Dr. Diane Stoler. Known by many as simply *Dr. Diane,* she is a respected psychologist from nearby Boxford, Massachusetts.

Like me, Dr. Diane is also a brain injury survivor. She was driving one night and experienced a stroke. Her injuries were far worse than mine. Dr. Diane worked hard at her own recovery and eventually made it back to her profession and resumed her work as a psychologist. After her stroke, her focus was quite different. She focused almost exclusively on working with people with brain injuries. Seeing what she did for herself gave me new hope. I hope that she would help me get my brain to work clearer, get me to college, help my athletic skills and help me to improve.

When I first started working with Dr. Diane, it easy as I knew I was in a bad place. I realized that therapy was necessary to me to get on with my life. I knew I needed help and that she, as a fellow brain injury survivor, knew what it would take to get me back on the right track. A couple of weeks turned into a couple months. A couple months then turned into a few years. She was instrumental in both my recovery and in helping me to attend Wheaton College.

After a year of ongoing therapy, I felt I had enough of her therapy and would always give my mother a hard time about going. Sometimes, if I knew I was going the night before, I would conveniently feel sick. "Mom, I don't think I can go to Dr. Diane tomorrow," I would call out, feeling more like a high school kid not wanting to attend class than the adult that I was. Soon enough, my mom got to know the routine. I would ask my mother, "What am I doing this for, no one else has to?" She would respond to it the same answer, "No one else you know was in a coma for three months either, you have to." She was stubborn and unwavering because she loved me. I understand that today.

Her comments quieted me down a bit but I still didn't enjoy going. Actually, I did like it when I finally got there, because I would walk out with a much clearer mind. For some reason, just getting there was hardest part for me.

After a few years, I started embrace therapy because I was seeing things about myself that were improving. For example, I didn't speak like I was drunk all the time because my brain was healing. Dr. Diane and my mother both told me that it would also help my baseball skills. That was something I really wanted to hear. The fact that my brain was getting better seemed inconsequential. I was walking, talking, going to the gym and playing the game I love. To me, that was all I need in my life to be happy.

Dr. Diane used neurofeedback therapy. She would hook me up to various wires and I would try to make things happen on the computer screen. I've always been competitive so when she would tell me to make the numbers go higher or lower I would concentrate and sure enough I could do it. Though I didn't really understand it at the time, I was actually retraining my brain. I was at a point before I started with her when I really had no short-term memory. After only six months of her therapy, my mother and I were leaving her house and I asked my mother a simple question. "What are we having to dinner?" Mom replied that we were having meatballs for dinner. "Mom, I had them for lunch." Now you have to understand that to a normal person, remembering meatballs for lunch is not really a big deal. But I wasn't anywhere near back to normal and I couldn't remember what I had done just an hour before. This was a huge breakthrough. Dr. Diane was exuberant. My mother and Dr. Diane were so excited that I remembered what I had for lunch. Something as simple as remembering meatballs became a turning point for me.

It became increasingly clear that the therapy was really working for me. I started to see measurable improvements in myself cognitively, socially and athletically. She helped speak without a slur and I began to do a lot more that my brain previously would not let me do. The process took me over three work-filled years.

Dr. Diane knows about brain injuries both from a clinical standpoint as well as a survivor standpoint. She is always discovering new and effective types of therapies to get the brain to work. She has a veritable toolbox of little gadgets and games that get your brain to think. She also stressed how important diet is to recovery. I stopped eating anything with sugar in it because I learned that sugar impairs your brain function. No more chocolate shakes for me! Most importantly, Dr. Diane helped me to regain my confidence.

I received many tough and hurtful comments from people I didn't even know about the little things that were wrong with me. I heard it at many different places from many different people. There are two circumstances that really come to mind.

Three years after my brain injury, I was working at Extra Innings where they were having a summer sports camp for young kids. I was helping out with the camp. A little boy asked me a question so I took the time to answer him. He looked away to the guys at the front desk and then looked back and said, "Are you retarded or something?" At that time it was very clear to others that I was having challenges. It was how my brain was functioning. Intensive therapy under the auspices of Dr. Diane therapy helped to rectify many of those challenges.

The most difficult incident and the one that made me feel the worst occurred when I went to a bar with some my friends in the summer of 2006. I don't drink alcohol but I went to a bar with them to have some very innocent fun. I choose not to drink because it almost killed me. Dr. Diane has shared with me that I can't drink as well.

"Your brain is already injured and alcohol will only bring further damage," she shared with me on several occasions.

I also have Epilepsy and alcohol will bring on seizures. Simply put, it's better that I abstain from alcohol. When I arrived at the front door of the bar, the bouncer wouldn't let me in at first. He thought I was already drunk because of the way I was talking. I then had to explain to him in front of everyone at the door why I talk the way I do, thinking that he would then let me in. All the bouncer did was embarrass me. When I told Dr. Diane about those two instances, she said to me, "You should just tell them to shut up, they don't know what it's like." Such is the candor from one survivor to another.

Anyone who gives me a hard time who doesn't know why I talk the way I do has no clue what I have been through and what I have had to deal with every day since 2003. Dr. Diane is right. Though they should say nothing because they don't know what it's like, their inappropriate responses are understandable.

Dr. Diane is also a sports psychologist and works with some professional athletes. One morning she told me Allan Houston was coming in to her office that day. He was an NBA star for the New York Nicks.

When I was done working with her, I came home, jumped on to my computer and printed out a picture of him to sign. I got a call from her a few hours later saying, "Allan is on his way." It was funny to me that she called him Allan, like he's just a regular guy.

When I met him, he was 6'8" and very nice. He gave me his autograph on the picture I brought in. He wrote his name like every autograph. Then he wrote in big quotes, "Trust Jesus," with a bible quote next to it.

Many professional athletes are quite religious. I have found that I am the same way. My first couple of years home found me hitting rock bottom. I became more religious than I ever was. I began to read the Bible and pray to God every night. I prayed not for myself but for the people who are having a harder time than I was. I was taught "If you believe that He will and you work hard at what you want than He will do all He can for you."

It sometimes takes a near death experience to make you change the way you think, to change your whole outlook on life. After my brain injury I definitely had a very different perspective on life. Every night lying in bed, I still pray for all the people I know and the people I met on my way back who are having a hard time. Belief and trust in higher power has done so much for me. It does so much for my life because I don't just think but I know I was saved for something great. Everyone is living on this earth for something.

I thank Dr. Diane for all the help she gave me as my recovery continued to progress. She not only helped get my brain ready for college, but helped me to regain faith in myself. This helped me become more independent, made me more sociable and helped my athletic skills as well. Like I have said before, your brain controls everything. I owe so much of who I have become to Dr. Diane.

I continued to work with her and true to form, I still complained all the time though only for the first three years because I was sick of all the therapies I was sent to and really wanted to get on with my life. However Dr. Diane explained to me that her therapy would help me get on with my life and I shouldn't fight it so much. It was many years after I started working with her when I began to see how much it did for me so I didn't complain, as much. In fact, by 2008 I started to regularly ask her when the next time I am going in to see her. By this time, I was seeing the positive affect it had on me and I wanted to see more. My mother was definitely surprised to see me actually want to go to therapy.

The biofeedback therapy Dr. Diane and I did together is without question the most boring thing I have ever done. I gave my mother a hard time whenever she brought me to work with her but that just turned into a habit. Because I complained so much about Dr. Diane my mother finally let me take a break from therapy. That didn't mean I would stop doing the bio feedback therapy though. Dr. Diane knew I needed it and shouldn't stop for any reason. She got it set up for me to do it at home. I did it for less than a year at home on my computer but my mother always urged me to go back. She told me that doing the biofeedback with Dr. Diane is more effective because her equipment is more powerful. When I went to Wheaton College and stopped doing the biofeedback, I saw, and most everyone close to me could see me start to slip. My speech started to slur again, my mind wasn't working as fast or as clearly as it was when I was seeing her and I felt my body and brain were not working together anymore. Because I could see those things happening I asked my mother if I could return to therapy. She was shocked but I think she knew I started to see what it was doing for me.

When I see her now I always ask if she still talks to or works with Allan Houston or any other professional athletes but she never gives me a straight answer. Maybe Michael Jordan? She laughs at my question. She started out as just my doctor. I am pleased that she is now my friend.

## Chapter Eleven

Everyone Needs Extra Innings

*"Just play. Have fun. Enjoy the game."*

*~Michael Jordan*

For my first three years home from of the hospital, I sat at home most of the day. When I wasn't in therapy, my dog Mugsy kept me company. At this point in time, I was quite angry about how my life was going and how much it had changed. I began to see where I was and knew where I should and wanted to be. Because of those feelings I felt that my life really was over and I didn't want to do anything. My mother told me I should get a job so I could get out of the house during the day. She also knew that sitting around by myself made me very depressed. Being my mother she saw those things happening and wanted to help me.

Being around baseball was one of the only things that made me happy. I was awarded *Massachusetts Baseball Player of the Year* after my senior year and then *Massachusetts Division Two Player of the Decade* for my hitting ability. Hitting was all I knew I was good at. After my brain injury I continued training to hit because I wanted to play shortstop again. I saw it as a challenge and because of that, I wanted it even more. Challenges drive me to do my best – even to this day. Though I am no longer a hitter on the baseball diamond I continue to go there to work on other things.

Extra Innings is a local sports training center that I've been going to just about every day since I was at a junior in high school. I remember going to hit nightly with my good friend and teammate, Adam. We have known each other since we were thirteen years old from playing on the same AAU baseball team together. Adam has always been a very hard worker and was my age so he was a good person to train with. Even after Adam graduated high school and was not playing college baseball, I was still able to give him a call and ask him meet me at Extra Innings. He always would. Without Adam to hit with every night I definitely would not have come close to the hitting skills I had when I was a senior in high school.

For many years after I was released from the hospital, Extra Innings always let me use their batting cages to hit for free. Pete was a coach of mine when I on the New England Mariner AAU team. He once played in the farm system for the Detroit Tigers and then got a job at Extra Innings. He gave me hitting lessons two times a week when I was in high school and then for a full two years afterwards.

At the end of 2004 I got a job at Extra Innings. Before I began working there, I really enjoyed just being there and liked all the guys there. Extra Innings helps me still because it is a place for me to work on my skills. It doesn't hurt that all the guys there let me use the facility for free. It was a place of camaraderie as I would make jokes about them but they always gave it right back.

By working at Extra innings I met many exceptionally nice people and it was really fun, at first.

It was baseball all the time and I loved going in to work because the other kids working with me were nice to hang out with. Lauren, who played softball at the University of Maine, became one of my closest friends.

But some of the people there were not so nice. This is hard to share, though I can now understand now why they were the way they were. It must have been frustrating working with me. I had a slur, memory problems and I repeated myself a lot. They didn't have the time to try to understand my hidden disability. Sadly, some treated me like dirt. Every day they had me do little jobs and thought that I wouldn't complain. They gave me small tasks like getting the coffee and cleaning trash in the woods. I was told that I couldn't talk to the customers, be at the desk or answer the phone because of my speech problems. This was not what I was expecting. I believe they only made me do it because they thought I wouldn't complain. They were wrong. That was one reason I had a bit of an unkind nickname for the place because some of the workers there were not nice people. While I do have a brain injury, I'm not stupid. I knew what was going on.

What was I getting paid to do? To get them coffee? Why was I working there in the first place? I couldn't understand. I knew they would give me a hard time about everything I did but it was a chance to get out of the house, make some money and better still, I could hit for free. I would get there early to hit before work and then after work and went back at night to hit some more. I would also hit with another player, Josh who was a senior in high school at the time. I hit with Josh every night in 2005. Lots of swings, and lots of great times.

As you might expect, working there didn't last long. The things they said to me and the way I felt I was treated was tough for me. They made me feel worthless. Realistically, who wants to feel that way? I can take a joke, believe me. We would laugh a lot, but it got to be out of hand. I was being joked a lot about things I could not control because of my brain injury. When a joke turns into a comment that really hurts someone it goes way too far.

Most people just don't understand what it's like, what it's like to be someone with a brain injury who hated their life. There are people who are very unsympathetic and don't care to understand the feelings of others. I felt I was trapped inside my brain and it didn't matter how hard I worked, I couldn't find my way out. There will always be certain people who don't take the time to understand, who put me down and think they are better than me because of the bad decision I made.

My mother had to pick me up from work every day and I would get in the car so mad, telling her how much I hated it. She listened to me and repeated told me I could leave as long as I got a job somewhere else.

When all the kids I enjoyed working with that summer went back to college, I decided to leave. That was also the time I started going to college myself, for the first time. It was when I went to Salem State College for one semester by taking one course in preparation to get ready for Wheaton College.

Even though I left Extra Innings as an employee, I still went there every single day to hit until the end of that summer. The attitude of those around me remained largely unchanged. They weren't mad that I left. Perhaps they were even a bit happy, but they still gave me a hard time about it. I have to say thank you to all the guys there for helping me get the best for my dream.

I think that was when things started to become a little calmer and when they started to be a little nicer to me. Every time I left I made sure to say thank you. Well sometimes, if I remembered. If that was all they wanted, I was happy to give it to them.

A personal thank you to all of the guys who helped me out at Extra Innings is very much in order. I will always be thankful for what they did for me during the years before and after my brain injury. So, to Pete, Mike, Rob, Kevin, Joe, Val, Sam, Lauren, Mr. Bevan, Veto, Scotty, Marsh, Josh and Dano, I say thank you.

## Chapter Twelve

## My Past Shaped my Future

*"Sometimes, things may not go your way, but the effort should be there every single night."*

~Michael Jordan

Looking back over my life, I now realize that my best friends today are the kids from my home town who I grew up with and went to school with from preschool through high school. Many of my closest friends lived across, behind or down the street from me. To this day, they continued to be the people I can count on. They were the only friends of mine who I was comfortable to call on a Friday or Saturday night to hang out with. They are my true friends and never made up an excuse not to see me.

I am so lucky to have friends like these in my life – friends who will always be there for me. I hope everyone can say they have friends who are there when you need them and will be there to support you in anything that you do. I thank them all for staying with me and not judging me or seeing me any differently after my brain injury.

When we all got to seventh grade things became a little different for us because at that time there were now kids from three different towns in our school. It was hard at first. Going into seventh grade was like going to preschool or kindergarten all over again - not knowing who was who or where to go. I did know a few others from playing on the all-star basketball team the year before. That took a bit of the pressure off.

One of the three towns was Topsfield, Massachusetts. Topsfield was not too rich but included families with some money and the type of kids in the town that made it the best place to grow up in. We were all the most down-to-earth kids you'd ever meet as we transitioned into seventh grade.

Boxford was different from the other two towns. They were all thought of as the rich kids of the school. They thought differently of themselves than most others thought of them. The basketball team I played on in sixth grade was where the best players from the three towns all played, but it may as well been a Boxford team. Not because we weren't good enough, but it was the Boxford players' fathers who coached the team. My Topsfield friends and I would get some minutes to play here and there but we mostly played the right side of the bench during those years.

The tides then turned when we all got to high school. The fathers couldn't coach so everyone had an equal opportunity. That was when I got the real chance to show who should have been playing.

The start of high school for me was the start of High school like it was for just about everyone else. Overall, I have to say that my high school years were much easier than I thought they would be. While I am intelligent, I need to share that I really just got by. "By the skin of your teeth," as my mother would say. I was accepted to several very good colleges, but obviously not for my academics.

Growing up I was always a year younger than everyone in my grade. That is why I graduated high school at seventeen while everyone else graduated at eighteen or nineteen. I never saw my age as a disadvantage. My baseball skills were better than kids in my grade and the grade above.

I was thirteen years old when I began my freshman year in the fall of 1998. I felt good about high school going in and was friends with a few upper classmen.

At the beginning of the academic year I was looking forward to the winter, looking toward the upcoming basketball season. When the basketball tryouts started, the coach split us up into two groups. The junior varsity and freshman all tried out together. The varsity team was made up of kids who played on the team the year before, some who played junior varsity and one freshman who was really ready to step up to varsity. That is usually how it goes for every sport. There is always one stand out freshman who you can't miss.

I made the freshman team my first year. In fact, all of my friends were put on the freshman team. It was nice as I didn't feel out of place and spent the whole season thinking about making the varsity team as a sophomore. I always look ahead and set very high standards for my performance. I do this to this day.

Looking ahead, I reasoned that the next year I would be bigger and stronger and I would have more of a chance to make the varsity team.

I decided not play the next year, however, because I didn't want anything to get in the way of my commitment to baseball. Looking back, it might have been best if I stuck with that plan.

By my junior year I had grown, was bigger physically and a lot tougher mentally. I went back and easily made the varsity basketball team. My baseball team had just won a state championship the previous spring so I was already on a good winning streak, but my basketball season that year we didn't do very well. Going 25-2 in baseball the season before as well as winning a state championship, I wanted to keep that winning streak alive. My basketball team did not have the drive it took to win, though we had some very talented players on the team. Because of my injury, I cannot remember much of high school but I do remember that season because of how many games we lost. I never had a season like that before and never want another one like that again. Our record ended sadly at 2-18.

I didn't know if I wanted to play basketball my senior year but I was named a captain so I thought I should play. That was yet another mistake. I was playing fall basketball with everyone on my high school team. During a game I was running to save a loose ball that was headed out of bounds and tapped it back in bounds. My momentum kept me moving forward. I was running fast and stuck my hand out to soften the blow of me hitting the wall. Without putting my hand out I would have hit the wall with my head. One more blow to my head - nothing I couldn't handle, at that time.

This left me with a broken wrist. I should have quit then, but after my wrist healed I came back and tried to play again. This time I was running to save a ball from going out of bounds. I didn't stick my hand out and hit the wall and dislocated my knee. Suffice to say, that was the end of basketball for me. I definitely wasn't going to ruin my chances to play baseball for a sport like basketball. Shared before, those who know me know that my lifelong idol is Michael Jordan. I realized Michael Jordan is not my idol because of what he did on the basketball court. He is my idol because of his competitive drive and what he did off the court to make him greater than the rest. I see him as the greatest athlete in history. I showed up to baseball tryouts not in the best of shape but I did what had to be done. I had to do what was expected of me, being a captain for the second year.

I have had many injuries in my life for a variety of different reasons and causes. I didn't let a torn ACL hold me back. I didn't let a broken wrist keep me down. I will not let a brain injury and ninety day coma stop me. That has been by far the hardest one of all to get through and overcome but I will am doing it. I have confidence that I will continue to thrive. Confidence is the key to success.

Playing sports play's a big role in social status in high school. I was a big time two-sport athlete, but it was baseball that I was best known for. Because the principal of my high school was the baseball coach, it made me very well-known by most teachers and students in the school. But being well-known does not stop life from happening. And life since high school is so much different than I ever expected. Most any brain injury survivor will tell you that.

## Chapter Thirteen

New Memories of a Past Life

*"I've never been afraid to fail."*

~Michael Jordan

It was in 2009 that I began to remember more and more about the years of my life that were once totally forgotten. It's strange to have entire blocks of time erased from your memory, but brain injury does strange things. During my freshman year I earned the starting third base job for the varsity team. The most amazing thing that happened that year was when I started at third base against Danvers High school at Lalachuer Stadium in the Massachusetts North finals of the state tournament.

My coach always believed in me because of the skill I showed, not because of how small I was. He had confidence to put me in the game in pressure situations. Being a freshman I was just starting my relationship with him. I always knew how great of a coach he was but I didn't know what a loyal guy he is until after I graduated high school.

In the spring 1999, my freshman year baseball tryouts came along. They were the hardest and most competitive I'd ever experienced. The coach knew how to win and that filtered down through our team. By the time I got there, the atmosphere about the team was a winning one.

Before tryouts the coach knew I was a good player. I was pretty small so I had to prove myself to him. I had to show him that my size wouldn't get in the way of my ability to compete and play with the best. Tryouts went great and things looked good.

I was invited back to the tryouts along with a few other freshmen who were good friends of mine. Coach Delani seemed to like me and I knew something great was in store. I felt I should make the varsity team because I knew I had the talent and would be a big part of helping the team to win. When the last tryout ended, Coach Delani took me aside and told me I made the Varsity team. I was so excited to play as a freshman and knew it was the start of something great. I was playing with kids who were eighteen while I was only fourteen.

Making the varsity team and starting as a freshman was also good because I felt a step above the other freshman. It seemed that at the start of the season something was missing from the team. The shortstop was a junior and the best player on the team so I knew I wouldn't play shortstop. At the beginning of the season during our scrimmages Coach Delani tried me out at second base but there was also a more talented senior there. So coach Delani chose to move me to third base where I stayed for the entire season.

I was weak and couldn't hit the ball very hard or far because I didn't yet have the muscle power. That was a bit of a joke on the team during my freshman year when we took batting practice. When I would get up to bat all of the players standing in the outfield would move up and stand in the infield. However I knew how to get guys in scoring position. This strategy put us in a position to win. I learned a lot that year about how to win and thank Coach Delani for teaching me.

My first year on the team was a great experience. I got to know and become friends with a lot of the older players as we would hang out before and after the practices and games. That helped me socially as well.

My team made it to the North Finals of the state tournament, four games deep into the tournament. We played at Lalacher Stadium in Lowell, Massachusetts. This wonderful park is a minor league park for the Boston Red Sox. We ended up losing the game 7-6 but what an amazing experience it was. Losing that game made the next year so much sweeter. Not too many kids can say they played in a game like that at such a young age. So my freshman season went great and things were only looking up.

The school year went okay but it was great in the spring because that was when I was at the top of my game on the field. When it came to school work, however, I wasn't nearly as competitive. I did just enough to get by, but baseball came before anything. If I had a chance to go to the batting cages and hit rather than do my homework, I always did. My grades never won me any awards but were always just good enough to play ball.

Throughout High School there are certain crowds you associate yourself with. For me, I was involved with the athletic crowd. Many of my best friends went on to play sports in college, sports like hockey, softball, baseball, basketball, football and lacrosse. One friend even signed a professional contract after college.

Some of us did separate by the time we got to high school but I think that is what friends do when they meet new people. It's part of the natural progression of life. Also, playing different sports usually affects who you hang out with and influences you. Because of that, the friendships that I had with my home town friends were not the same in high school because some of us didn't play the same sports.

When I was in high school I would drink on weekends with my friends like many high school students do. It was by the end of my senior year that I was drinking too much. This might be the reason I am in the position I am in today and the reason I am writing this. Although I was told that it could have also been a seizure that night.

After I graduated, a few of my close friends got on the wrong track. The people they got involved with got them into doing very addictive drugs. I was taught early in my life that drugs won't help you achieve anything. Drugs only set you back. Taking any kind of drug is something I have never been into because any drug will affect the way I lived and played ball. Especially now, seeing how my brain has already been damaged.

"You have been my best friend since we were in fourth grade and I would do anything for you," my friend Tim shared at one point after my accident.

Tim and I separated a little during high school and today I wish we hadn't. I now see that there are the people in my life who will do anything for me, as I will for them. I hope everyone growing up has friends in their life that they can count on and know they will always have someone to be there for them. I wouldn't trade their friendship for anything. They all helped me so much through the toughest years of my life.

When I woke up and wasn't who I used to be. Most of my old friends had vanished. It's sad and very hard for me when I think about it. They never made an effort to come around to see me when I was first home and the years following. Sometimes I ask myself if I was really friends with them in the first place. I know today that friends very often step away from brain injury survivors. It's a very common and well-documented occurrence. This doesn't make it easier, just understandable.

Friends are something everyone needs in their life. Without someone to pick you up when you fall, you would stay down. I have had many friendships with many different types of people throughout my life, but the most important ones to me were always there for me.

The friends you have now, ask yourself if they are good or bad friends. I realized after 2002 that most of the friendships I made in high school were just that, friends from high school. I can think of a few who stayed around, who talked to me and kept me up when I felt I hit rock bottom. But the rest left when it got hard. Everyone who stayed, kept me up and kept me focused when I was really thinking about running into traffic, I know will be my friends forever.

My first and my best friend in the world, Brooke wrote this to me. I will never forget it.

*"Your heart has always been put into everything you do from sports to even playing house when we young. We had the best of times and they will never leave my heart. I will never forget all you have done for me. You easily are the nicest, most genuine, down to earth kid I know and I will continue to know that for the rest of my life. I love you Tim like a brother and your heart and soul are strong enough to get through any challenges that come your way. I am here for you no matter what"*

If I knew what would happen after 2002 I would definitely change the crowd I was involved with at that time. I think I was part of what some might call the "athletic cool popular crowd." But what exactly does that mean? Because my high school was a three-town high school there were a lot of kids with many different meanings of what it means to be "cool."

If you are good at sports, does that make you "cool?" If you are dating the most popular girl, does that make you "cool?" When I was the best baseball player in the state and had so many friends how "cool" was I? When I had a full athletic scholarship to college I must have been "cool," but then how "cool" was I when I went into my coma, released from the hospital and came home in 2003? I wasn't, "cool" anymore. In my mind's eye, I became a nobody, a nobody no one wanted to be around.

One of the friends who left told me, "It's too hard, things will never be the same." She was right. Today, I don't want things to be the same. I have learned that everything happens for a reason and I am blessed to still be able to play the game I love. I have learned so much since my life changed forever. Those are valuable lessons and something everyone should think about.

All friendships are different. It depends on the loyalty they have to you. Earlier I mentioned the blue notebook that I was given in 2003. Everyone who came to the hospital to see me wrote in it. I read it every night for the four years before I got to Wheaton College. I read it cover to cover hundreds of times. It's sad as most of the kids who wrote in that book were so worried and cared so much for me. They did not live up to what they told me. I don't know why I kept reading it and always wondered why so few of my best friends from my home town ever came in or wrote in that notebook.

In fact, there were two from Topsfield who came in everyday and wrote in it all the time. One of my best friends Mike did. He went to a community college that was close by. The other was Brooke because we have known each other and been best friends since early childhood. They would write funny stories about things that happened when we were young. Reading these messages and stories was good for my memory. If I could remember those times than more memories would eventually come back. I also learned a lot about myself and the trust I should give to others. Some people who I was not very close with, I became closer with afterwards.

*"Tim, I want you to know that I didn't go into the hospital because I knew you would be okay, all of us from Topsfield have known you the longest and we all knew you would wake up and be fine. I didn't want to see you like that because I never knew you like that. I know how strong you are and I know you well enough to know you would wake up, no one has a heart like you. I didn't know why everyone was so worried."*

My friend Todd made this note in my blue notebook. He was the only person who I grew up with that I had the guts to ask. I felt I didn't need to ask any of the others because I knew I would get the same response. My hometown friends are the friends of mine who know me for me, knew I would be fine and continued to be my best friends afterwards because they knew I wouldn't change. It is clear to me that they will forever be there for me when I need them just like I will always be there for them. I was blessed to grow up where I did and make the friendships I did when I was so young.

His comment meant more to me than anyone who wrote things in a book that they didn't mean and did not do. I will remember what he said to me for the rest of my life. After that night I understood why they didn't want to come in to see me. Who wants to see one of their best and long-time friends in the hospital the way I was?

They all know me for the nice, strong and good person I am and stayed with me for the stronger person I have become. Todd helped me feel more comfortable about my whole situation and gave me more respect for them all. He also gave me more confidence in myself. "It's our turn to be here for you and we're here the whole way," Todd shared later.

*"I've known you since fourth grade, for nine years. I'd have to say you're one of my best friends in the world. If I were to write some of our memories, I wouldn't be writing enough, but if I wrote everything I'd be writing for the rest of my life. So I'm going to leave that up to you because we both know the memories. You're going to come out of this. It's a long road but I'm here with you from beginning to end. I just want you to know that we have more memories to make Tim. You're a tough son of a bitch Tim, don't*

*give up. Love you more than you'll ever know dude, Mike"*

My best friend in high school, Mike, wrote this to me. And the appreciation I have for the truly meaningful relationships in my life is so much more than it has ever been. My brain Injury made me a stronger person.

## Chapter Fourteen

We Get by With a Little Help from our Friends

*"Champions do not become champions when they win an event, but in the hours, weeks, months and years they spend preparing for it. The victorious performance itself is merely a demonstration of their championship character."*

~Michael Jordan

After I was released from the hospital, it took time for me to get back on my feet and back on the baseball diamond but I was determined to do so. I had to show myself and others that I could still play at the highest level. After what I went through since my brain injury I honestly believe that I can do anything.

Everything I do now turns into a competition and I put in everything I have so I will win. I won early on in my life by using my skill. Later on I learned the mentality you need to win from Michael Jordan as well as from my high school baseball coach, Peter Delani. It didn't matter to me that Michael Jordan played basketball. He worked harder than anyone and won because of it. That is what I took from him – his drive to win. This is a big part of why he has always been my idol and a driving force to help me to succeed.

To overcome the challenges in life that we all face, you need motivation, determination as well as the desire to work hard. Luckily I must have been born with a heart like a lion!

I have had to overcome many other challenges in my life and my brain injury is yet another opportunity for me to prove what I am capable of doing. Attitude is all about using your heart, determination and desire to prove that you can do the things people think you can't or are no longer capable of doing.

My brain injury is nothing but another life challenge - a challenge to show what I can do in the face of tremendous adversity. I will never quit. Michael Jordan said, "Quitting is for losers and I don't think anyone on this earth wants to be known as a loser." I couldn't agree more.

It was in 2004 when I went to Salem State to take a few courses to get prepared for my studies at Wheaton College. However it was really hard to get through courses because my memory was very bad. I just couldn't concentrate and focus on school work. I wanted to get done with it so I could head to the gym and the batting cages.

Not only was my memory at its worst but my social skills were also not where they should have been. My mother was working so I would get picked up on the days I had class from, "The Ride." I always got there to school without any issues, but one day I didn't make it home for a few hours after my last class was over.

After my class that day, I walked outside and saw a bus that looked like the bus I always took to get there. I got on it thinking it would take me home, but that's not even close to what happened. I was on the bus with many different people I didn't know – people who I thought they were going home as well. It took me two hours to realize I was on the wrong bus. Sitting on the bus, I thought, "Didn't we already pass this spot?" that I remember seeing that twenty minutes ago. My mother called me asking me where I was. "I don't know mom. I think I have passed fitness center a few times now." She suggested I speak with the bus driver. The driver didn't give me an answer that I could understand so I called my mother back. "The bus driver said he is going to Topsfield after a few more stops but I have been on here for so long, I don't know what's going on".

My mother asked if it said The Ride on the side of the bus. It became clear that I had boarded the wrong bus. The driver said that it wasn't, "The Ride" and he wasn't going to Topsfield. Looking back, I see that he must have thought I had some serious issues. In frustration, I called my mother back and she told me to get off at the next stop and that my Dad would come get me. I got off the bus in the middle of the city of Salem. I was mad at myself and mad at the bus driver for not telling me I was on the wrong bus.

I got in the car with my father and he said, "Didn't you realize you were on the wrong bus after passing the same place a couple times?" I felt so stupid that I lied and said that someone told me it was the bus for me so I got on it. I didn't know it would take me around for two hours.

My father was not mad at me. Rather, he was mad at the bus driver for not noticing that I was on the bus for so long and not asking me where I was going. That was when I thought to myself that I really needed my license back or get someone to drive and pick me there so I wouldn't do that anymore. I had enough of being frustrated at this type of transportation.

It was Coach Delani who helped me again. He got a former player of his, Ben, to be my tutor. It wasn't hard to see why. Ben is a Harvard Graduate and was home during the winters because he was playing professional baseball in the farm system for the Colorado Rockies. When Ben played at my high school he was the first player to be named a two-year captain and to get his number retired when he graduated. Ben is someone I always knew about and looked up to. I was also named a two-year captain and when I graduated Coach Delani retired my number just like he did for Ben. I was so excited to work with him.

Having Ben as my tutor was the best think that could have happened at that time. He would come over in the morning and we would go to the library down the street from my house. Not many people can say that they've had a Harvard graduate and semi-pro ball player as their tutor. After studying for a couple hours we then went to the gym. At the gym Ben had me do workouts from the Colorado Rockies. That was our daily routine until one fated day.

Because of my memory problem, one morning I forgot to take my seizure medicine. Ben and I went to the library and everything was fine. We then went to the gym and things were still going well, at least at first. The last thing I remember was lifting on the bench. Things suddenly went dark. I woke up in an ambulance on the way to the hospital. The paramedic was leaning over my stretcher saying, "You had a seizure and we are on our way to the hospital."

I talked to Ben the next day and he told me that he didn't know what I was doing. He said I dropped the dumbbells and started looking to the sky and then just fell to the ground and started shaking. I am told that is what I do before a seizure occurs. I start looking to the sky. After that day I only worked with Ben for one more week. He was still playing for the Rockies and had to return to spring training. When Ben left, he helped me even more by giving me the Colorado Rockies workouts. But just going to the gym and telling people, "Look at this, this is from the Colorado Rockies," well, this was pretty cool.

I felt I was on my way. If you put your mind to something and work hard, when you get a chance to perform you can do anything. I can think of so many athletes who have proved that over and over.

Michael Jordan showed this. Roger Clemens was forty-four and still played professional baseball. Tom Brady was given a shot by the New England Patriots look at what he has done since -  three super bowl wins in four years is something never seen before.

Yes, let's get back to Michael Jordan again. You're probably saying to yourself, "Ok now you're going a little far." He said everyone doubted him when he decided to go to North Carolina to play basketball. "Everyone expected me to go to North Carolina, sit on the bench for a year then come home and work at a local gas station or something." You know the rest and why he is a legend and my idol and why I have looked up to him for my entire life. I believe he has taught me more about life than just sports. I know today that there is more to life than just sports.

## Chapter Fifteen

Moving Along

*"My heroes are and were my parents. I can't see having anyone else as my heroes."*

~Michael Jordan

In 2005 my mother, my sister and I moved to nearby Middleton, Massachusetts to live with David, my mother's fiancé. He had just retired and bought a beautiful home. I enjoyed it but it was really weird at first, not living in Topsfield for the first time in my life. When they got engaged he told my mom that she could retire also. That was a good thing for her because she works so hard in everything she does, especially getting me back to a normal life again. She deserved a break.

We sold our house in Topsfield, she retired and it looked like everything would be great for the rest of her life. But time was about to show that wasn't to be the case. The time I spent in Middleton was a good time. Even though it didn't work out, my mother liked being with her fiancé at the time so she was happy. My mother being happy is all I want for her because she has done so much for me. If she is happy, then I am happy. She also made a real good friend while living in Middleton - her best friend, Val.

She met Val when we moved in. Even after we moved out Val continued to be her best friend. When I met Val for the first time, my mom and I were walking home and she said to me, "You know Val is eighty-eight years old." I was so surprised when she said that. Val was the most upbeat person and looked like she was in her fifties. Val would come over to my house occasionally and I would see her around every so often. After a year of living in Middleton, my mother told me that it was Val's eighty-ninth birthday. At that time I didn't have a car or any money. I decided to write her a poem.

My mind was still a little off but it was getting clearer every day. I thought she would enjoy a poem from me, rather than a gift - because it would come right from my heart. So I wrote her a poem, my mom went to her house the next day for her birthday dinner and gave it to her. When my mom came home she said to me, "Val started to cry when she read it." Having my mother tell me that made me feel so good that I could make Val so happy because being so good to my mother she really meant a lot to me.

Moving was a good thing in the beginning because my mom works so hard in everything she does, especially getting me back to a normal life again. She deserved a break. It was only a short break but I think she enjoyed that little time off. After she retired I could tell that she missed working. She missed not getting up and doing something every day and missed the people who she worked with the most.

After two years my mother realized she wasn't as happy as she thought she would be. Because of that we moved again, to the next town over, Danvers, and she went to back to work.

Leaving Middleton after only two years was just another move. I missed seeing Val every day and my mom did too. I would also miss everything that went along with living in Middleton, like the indoor pool I used to increase the strength in my legs. After we left, Val would still invite my mom and me over some days just to chat. She also let me use the indoor pool there during the first winter after we left Middleton.

One morning on my way out the door I forgot to take my seizure medication. I met up with Val, got the key to the pool and started doing my leg exercises in the water. I did all the exercises I needed to do and then got in the hot tub to relax and stretch my muscles. I was in the hot tub for ten minutes when my next seizure struck. I again opened my eyes lying on the ground with paramedics all around me.

"You had a seizure and we are going to take you to the hospital."

I was coughing up water for a week but I thought to myself later, "At least I got all my exercises done." I'm very lucky there was a man in the other room who saw me. He knew who I was, saw me go under and not come up for a couple minutes so he ran out to the pool area to see what I was doing.

Thank God for that guy because if he didn't see me go under and not come up I would not be here today. Suffice to say, that was the last time Val let me use the pool. She didn't want anything to happen because of something she did for me.

During the summer of 2007, I played a baseball game in my hometown. Val came to the game with my mother to watch me pitch. When the game was over Val started talking to a few friends of mine on my team and everyone loved her. She was joking around with one of my teammates and a longtime friend. We went to eat down the street and I said to him,

"You know it's her 90th birthday today?"

Right away he said to me, "Shut up, are you kidding me, she doesn't even look sixty."

Val passed away in 2009. I still miss her and think of her every day.

Even though Middleton did not work out for us as a family, leaving Topsfield was just what I needed. It was my home for twenty years. It was there that I had the best of times but also the worst of times. I spent the first three years out of the hospital there and thought I would be stuck there forever. Living in Middleton also didn't work out, but I strongly believe that everything happens for a reason. I can now say that today with the sincere honesty.

Maybe I went into a coma for a reason. Some may feel that's going a little far, but I know I woke up for a reason. I never thought of things that way until I got to know Father Mike. Father Mike was the brother of my mother's co-worker. He would always come by to see me at Spaulding and we became good friends. He would tell me that everyone is born with a purpose and that is why we are here. We weren't born just to live but to carry out what we were put here to do. It sometimes takes a near death experience to make you think that way. After my brain injury I definitely thought that way. I know how much worse it could have been for me, after seeing and meeting the people I have. It does so much for my life because I don't just think but I know I was saved for something great. Everyone is living on this earth for something.

# Chapter Sixteen

Hello Wheaton College!

*"Sometimes you need to get hit in the head to realize that you're in a fight."*

~Michael Jordan

By the time 2006 rolled around, I was ready to go to Wheaton College, or at least I thought I was. Had it not been for my accident, Wheaton College was the school I was supposed to go after I graduated high school. I liked the school and I liked the baseball coach. Thankfully, my dream of getting there to play baseball was still intact.

It was during my junior year of high school that I started to get college and professional baseball recruiting letters from schools all around the country. But I had committed to Coach Podbelski at Wheaton College. Looking back, I now realize that I just wanted to play ball and I was guaranteed a starting shortstop position at Wheaton.

Academically, school was never on my high list of priorities. If I had been a random applicant to Wheaton College with no baseball background, I certainly would not have been accepted. Coach Delani helped me by talking to their coach and getting everything set up for me to go. After my brain injury, the Wheaton administration told me that whenever I was ready and able to handle the school work that I would be reaccepted. Coach Delani, Dr. Diane and my mother were three people who never gave up on me. They did all they could to help me to achieve my goal. Getting to Wheaton College was my goal for four years because no one thought I could. I was not going to stop until I got there.

I was told by a professional scout, after he saw me throw, "It is your dream and no one else's, don't let anyone take your dream away from you. Don't ever give up because it's never too late."

What he said gave me confidence and is something that kept me working hard. I will do the impossible, I have to.

Every day I worked to be a hitter because that was what everyone told me I couldn't do so. This made me want to succeed even more. When I arrived at Wheaton College in 2006 I changed my whole attitude about the game

My friend Baker and I were going to the same college. We would hit and lift everyday together to play the field. He also became strictly a pitcher when he got to college and was then signed by the San Diego Padres. Baker getting signed to a professional team was yet another example that if you work hard for what you want, never give up, you can do anything.

If I went to Wheaton College in 2002 who knows what would have happened. Being a shortstop and playing up north where it isn't as competitive as it is down south, I don't think I would have achieved my dream but who really knows. What I do know is that I enjoyed what I did at the time and was the best at what I did so I didn't want to stop.

My message to everyone who is involved in sports is this: If you think you can make it to play at a higher level or simply want to play at a higher level, listen to yourself and do what you think is best for you. It is your life and you know yourself best. Don't listen to people who put you down and tell you that you can't do something you want to do.

I have had people in my life since 2002 that were and still are that way towards me. Some think I should basically go sit in a room and stare at a wall for the rest of my life because I got and I could get, "hurt." You can get hurt doing anything, even crossing the street. If you believe in yourself, work hard and stay positive. Never give up and keep chasing your dream. If you have a dream, it is your dream.

Belief in yourself and never giving up are two valuable lessons I have learned. I guess I had to relearn them. The belief I have in myself got me to where I am today and will get me to where I want to go. It has taken me farther than I ever thought I would get to.

I don't care if some have been there for me or not but the people I have in my life today are the people I need because they are all positive and believe in me. They like me for the person I am now, not for who I used to be. I am given confidence so I can get up every day and keep going in the positive direction I am going in.

High school was always fun because I was a well-known athlete and a popular student. When arrived at Wheaton College I felt like a nobody. I liked my baseball teammates because they knew what it took for me to get there and they respected me for it. Some kids at the school heard the way I talked and wanted nothing to do with me. It wasn't because of the students that I eventually left Wheaton. It was more but because of the school work. Winning for me in school meant passing grades.

I did leave Wheaton College after working for four years to get there but that was just something life gave me. I had to learn to live with it. I had to find another way. I am playing the cards I was dealt as best I can. School work is something I can't do anymore but that didn't mean I would quit my dream.

My mother shared with me,   "Tim, you've come so far and worked so hard, you have to find another way of life, it can't be school but there are other things you can do, there are other ways to capture your dream. Go and find it!"

I was given the people and the strength I need by putting her in my life. She gives me strength and confidence to do what no one thinks can be done: to come back, play the game I love and live a normal life again.

In the middle of my one semester at Wheaton College, I started to feel more comfortable in the classroom and at the school every day. I wrote how I had to make my mother proud because she helped me the most to get to where I was, where I am and helps me get to where I want to go. I am blessed with the heart and the strength to overcome anything. I cannot let my mother down. I will forever work hard to make her proud.

The reason I decided to go to Wheaton College while I was getting letters from many other schools all over the country was because it was a good academic school. It never hurt that they had a successful baseball program and guaranteed me a starting shortstop position. I wanted it even more after my coma because no one thought I would be able to make the baseball team. After being readmitted to

Wheaton, making the baseball team was the next challenge I had to overcome.

Everyone thought my playing days were over but that was far from the truth. Getting back on the baseball field and attending Wheaton College were my biggest goals at that time. I overcame a lot before I was due to start at Wheaton, so I wasn't going to let this one slip by. Wheaton College is a tough and a very expensive school and my mother was on her own paying for me to go. Knowing how expensive it was, I was surprised she still wanted me to go. She only wanted it for me because she knew I wanted it. My mother does everything she can to support me and found a way for me to attend. My grandparents helped too. Thank God for family.

When I arrived at Wheaton College in the fall of 2006 I didn't know what to expect. I was a little nervous because I didn't know anyone going in. At the time, I still didn't talk very clearly. After hearing all the hurtful comments from people before I got to college about the way I did talk, I was scared that all the students at the school would make the same unkind accusations about me. I was afraid of accusations that I was stupid, drunk or had a serious problem. My social skills were not the best so meeting people and making friends was something I was afraid of.

I was nervous how the kids at the school might judge me because of how I spoke and maybe how I acted. When I arrived at Wheaton, my memory was still pretty bad. If I didn't write everything down I would soon forget it. My memory was pretty much stolen from me on the night of my accident. A pen and paper is how I made up for it. I see it as a story like, "David vs. Goliath" a little bit. This was something that I wrote in my journal the first day I got to Wheaton College. It was me against the world.

Because of my poor memory, I carried around a book to write my schedule for the day. Trying to remember names is very hard for me as well. In the back of that book I carried, I wrote down the names of everyone who I met at my freshman orientation. Right next to their name I would write a characteristic about them. For most people I would just write something simple. If someone was tall, short, funny but sometimes I would ask the people what I should write about them.

I will never forget Gabby, and what she said when I asked her what to write. She was a senior helping with freshman orientation. She was very nice to me so I wanted to write something nice about her. I thought I would write "Nice," but she said, "No, what do you really think of me?" I started to get nervous and said, "Funny?" Then she said, "Wicked hot". From then on her name to me became the wicked hot girl. I started laughing and I will never forget her for that. She didn't think of me as weird because I had to carry around a book to remember. She became one of my best friends there, someone I ate dinner with every night and someone who I continue to talk to, even today. She graduated the year I left and is now working with kids like myself, kids with brain injuries. When she told me what she was doing I thought it was awesome because it shows how open-minded of a person she is.

At school, I started to type a journal so I would know what I did the previous day without asking people. I would write down how my classes were going. If I was having a hard time, how I felt about the classes, the work I was given and the people I met. I wrote as well about the baseball team because baseball was the real reason I was attending. It was interesting to me when I read what I wrote in my journal when I came home. I wrote that I was starting to see my brain injury as more of a challenge than anything else. I still think that way today.

Being at Wheaton College the first few days was very hard. It was a type of atmosphere I was not used to - living on a college campus and taking more than one class. I thank everyone I met while I was there for making my transition to college and my experience there so much fun. I had to find different ways to get things done. I wasn't the smart kid I was when I woke up from my coma. Because of that, when I got to college I had to find other ways to do well. I had to find people to help me because I couldn't do the work on my own. I was developing compensatory strategies and didn't even realize it.

Wheaton College is not a big school and is pretty easy for most people to find their way around. Not so for me. Every morning and afternoon I had to call my mother for help. I had to ask her about my class schedule, what time I was meeting my tutor and where my classes were. I didn't want to ask any of the students because I didn't want to look stupid. My tutor Alison and I met every day and the administration had me work with "The Office for Students with Disabilities." I was allowed to take only two courses while everyone else had to take four. The NCAA also gave me permission to play baseball with only two classes.

Alison didn't really understand how a brain injury affects someone but she did try hard to understand my challenges. She wanted me to quit baseball and spend all of my time on school work. In hindsight, she was probably right. She didn't understand that my real goal was to play baseball at Wheaton College. To be honest, I could have spent 100% of my time studying but when you have significant issues with memory, it is like fighting a losing battle.

She did help a lot and helped me to get through the first semester. When we first started to meet, she contacted all of my professors and wanted to create a "Tim Team" so everyone would know how I was doing. Some of the professors were willing to do this, but many were not. The Wheaton College administration wouldn't let it happen saying that it would be too much trouble for the professors. So Alison had to rely on what I told her, which was not an easy task for her because of my memory issues. Alison made notebooks for each of the classes I was taking. My notebooks had different folders labeled, "Notes from the class"  "Homework" and "Class Work." They did help, but for me it was still very difficult. My classes were just too hard for me. I would take in the information but I would just have trouble remembering it. The school was not helpful or cooperative and would not help me even though they knew from the beginning of my disability. It became quite clear they weren't used to having a student with a brain injury. They were totally against me and the limitations I faced. But I did make it through one semester with a passing grade!

At the end of the first couple months at Wheaton College, I remember lying in my bed wanting to die for getting myself in the situation I was in.  I read that when I got home and I do remember lying in my bed thinking that way and saying those things to myself. How I wished I didn't live through my coma because anything would have been better than the way I was feeling and I thought if I died it would have been better. It was dark thinking indeed.

Looking back, it's easy to get mad at myself. Today, I can't believe I would ever think that way. Why should I feel bad for myself when I have it good compared to the people I have met since my accident as well as so many others around the world?

When baseball started that fall, I was a little nervous but so excited to finally be playing on a college team. I was realizing a goal of mine from when I woke up from the coma, a goal that I was told it was impossible. This was the team I worked so hard to play for. During my first game the coach put me at third base. That was good for me because I played that position for my first two years in high school. In the second inning it came time for my first at bat. I was on deck looking forward to showing everyone what I could do. I got to bat... ball 1, strike 1. The next pitch came up and in and hit me right in the head. Everyone got nervous and the coach told me, "You are just a pitcher now." That was okay with me because with my height, leg and arm strength, I knew that I would be able to help the team more that way, providing they gave me the chance.

It was the beginning of the second semester when things really started to fall apart. Every week, twice a week, pitchers participated in morning running. One morning I was in a hurry to get there, rushing to get my bag together and my baseball stuff on. I was in such a hurry that I left my room without taking my seizure medicine.

I arrived at the gym and started running with my teammates. It was maybe two or three laps in when all of sudden I woke up on a stretcher. Unknown to me, I had a seizure and scared my teammates half to death. I was told I started running in the middle of the basketball court, looking to the sky, doing circles and just fell and started shaking. That was my second seizure at Wheaton College. They now looked at me as a liability.

Our spring baseball trip to Arizona was coming up in March of that year and I was told I couldn't go. I went into Boston to see my doctor and got permission to play, as they requested, so I could go on the trip with the team. But the administrators at Wheaton didn't care. They didn't want me to go. This was extremely upsetting for me but they would not reconsider it. My mother went down to talk to them but they had already made up their minds. The staff at the school knew I had a brain injury, knew the school work would be a hundred times harder for me than it would be for anyone else and they used my seizure as an excuse. Frankly, I don't even know why they reaccepted me.

So I came home after a few days after starting the second semester. I had taken a school loan for that semester and even though I had only been there a few days they would not forgive the loan. They weren't willing to help but that didn't stop them from taking the money. Knowing how expensive the school is and how much time I had spent working to get there, I felt my life had shattered again. I made the tough decision to not go back to Wheaton. Would I even have graduated if I stayed? My answer to that question was not a no, but a probably not. My baseball coach never even said goodbye to me. I became depressed and angry again.

However, I made four real good friends at Wheaton College who are still a big part of my life today. I will always remember what Lap, Marty, Simmons and Gabby did for me when I was at Wheaton College and how they treated me with respect and dignity and how they made me feel when I was around them. They made the short time I spent there so much easier.

# Chapter Seventeen

## The Sky is my Limit

*"If you're trying to achieve, there will be roadblocks. I've had them; everybody has had them. But obstacles don't have to stop you. If you run into a wall, don't turn around and give up. Figure out how to climb it, go through it, or work around it."*

~Michael Jordan

When I came home, I didn't know what I was going do with my life. My mother then brought up the idea of me going to Curry College as an older cousin of mine went there. Curry has more help for people with my challenges. Curry College seemed like the new place for me to be. In April of 2007 after going to see the school and talking with them they chose not to accept me.

I later read in my journal that things were going well the first month at Wheaton, but then the work load just got to be too much. My classes were too hard because there was so much reading and writing and all the while I was forgetting to do things. My memory problem made me fall behind. This was yet another reason I chose to leave. I tell people it was my seizure during morning running but when I read my journal that was not the only reason. You know what they say about hindsight.

Life was not going well. "Why did I wake up?" I asked myself repeatedly. I had to keep going and do something with my life to show no matter what happens to you, you can overcome anything and do what you want. With the right attitude and if you believe in yourself, it's amazing what you can do. You also need the right people in your life because without them I wouldn't be where I am today.

I am an extremely motivated person, especially after all I have overcome. I know I will get to show the truth, the truth about everything I have mentioned. You need, heart, courage and lots of determination. Whether you're up or you're down, whether your brain injured, severely injured or paralyzed, you need the right people in your life because without them you would go nowhere, I would be nowhere.

After the Wheaton experience, I was scared that I would never find another job or another girlfriend. I applied to a few places and with help from the Massachusetts Rehab Commission I had a few different jobs but I was always let go because of my brain injury. They said it was because they were nervous I would "hurt" myself. Through Mass Rehab, I got a job working in the kitchen for an elderly assisted living home. My counselor wanted to be my job coach to help me get the routine down. They wouldn't let her come. As you can well imagine, that job didn't last very long. It was beginning to appear that whatever I tried to do was not working. But I was not willing to give up.

In the fall of 2007 I went back to Salem State College to give it yet another try. I wanted to graduate from somewhere because I felt that is what everyone does in life. People go to college after high school, they get a college degree and they start a life. I lived on campus with a roommate and tried to fit in. I played on the baseball team too. But more seizures ruined my chance to finish there as well. I had a tutor, Lenore, who helped me get through a semester. Sadly, she got very impatient with me as my memory challenges became clear. School work was obviously not my priority, playing baseball was. She got mad at me after I missed a few of our meetings because she thought I wasn't trying. I did try but it didn't show because I wasn't focused on my class work.

Around this time, I began to think about getting a "seizure dog." Better still, the Massachusetts Brain Injury Association was going to pay for it. Seizure dogs are amazing and can really help people who have a seizure disorder like the vets coming home from Afghanistan and Iraq. These amazing dogs are trained to know when you are about to have a seizure. Everywhere I go people know my situation and know what to do if I do have a seizure. Seizure dogs are "service dogs" so they are allowed to go anywhere with you. When I asked the owner of my gym and the owners of the batting cages if I would be able to bring it in they said quite clearly that I couldn't. They said a dog was a liability. Even though I was told that is illegal not to allow me in with a "service dog," I thought I was a liability enough for them. It was just a roadblock I had to get through. Experience has shown me that I am good at working through roadblocks.

The reality is that I wasn't really responsible enough to take care of a dog at that time. Since then my seizures have been under control with a Proshi machine, a small personal machine invented by Chuck Davis from California. I put it on a table in my bedroom at night. It sends out preprogrammed light frequencies through a pair of glasses. I can't really explain how or why it works but it certainly does. I still have to take my seizure medication but the dosage has dropped significantly so I have fewer side effects from the drugs. It's easy and painless – when I remember to turn it on.

I knew I was given back life and my ability to be able to play the game I loved for a reason. I also know I am being lead in the right direction. I know my life was saved by someone and that someone has not left my side once since my accident. The days I was unconscious in the hospital, I was kept breathing by a machine. I continue to work to be the best on the baseball diamond again. I know the one who saved my life will help me do it. Unfortunately, not everyone sees it that way.

From my hard-fought life experiences and what I have been taught, I have learned that you need to follow your dreams and never give up. With hard work, determination, commitment and dedication you can do anything. It's not always easy. As a matter of fact, it is never easy. I work hard for everyone who has helped me get to where I am today. Some of my friends and my entire family have given me what I need to get back so I will thrive again. With the negativity I have been around I continue to follow my heart because the people who know me the best give me confidence in myself.

Many people have been there for me over the years. Not just the people there when I was in the hospital, but many more who I have gotten closer to when I was back on my feet. I am so thankful to all the positive people who are in my life today who all supported me and helped me from day one. They all gave me encouragement which gave me motivation and made me believe in myself.

I became friends with so many different people since my brain injury. I have learned a lot about who to and who not to trust because of my experience. Many perceived friends of mine turned their backs when I returned home from the Middleboro Greenery. For those who did, I am glad that they did because I can't have negativity in my life. I have learned that positive thinking will take you farther than you've imagined.

There are feelings I had about myself and the chances that I was given, which was no chance. Not just a chance on the baseball diamond but chance's with the friends I lost. My brain injury showed me many things about who I am.

I've been at some of the worst places and seen people with problems that you can't even imagine. I have learned to respect people, especially those who have no control over how they act and what they can or cannot do. I have met those types of people and know they are just like everyone else only with problems they can't do anything about. Because of that there is no reason to dislike or think any less of them for the things they can't control. What happened to them was not in their life's plans, just like what happened to me was not in mine.

I have seen people with half of their head taken off so they live their life with white bandages covering their head. I learned to love life and do as much as I can with the life I was given back because I know what I could be like and where I could be. I was given a second chance and that second chance I was given so that I will do something great with it.

After what I have gone through and overcome I now live with the mindset of, "The sky is my limit." Everyone playing a sport has to live by the phrase, "I will never be beat." If you play and live with that mindset, you will have more confidence in yourself and your abilities will show through. You have to believe in yourself. Anyone is capable of anything. So many of the people I have met since my brain injury prove that every day.

I now live in the world I got myself into and I work hard every day to live it to the best of my ability. I will never give up on my dreams. I stay positive. To thrive, you must stay positive.

## Chapter Eighteen

### Lessons to Live By

*"If you're trying to achieve, there will be roadblocks. I've had them; everybody has had them. But obstacles don't have to stop you. If you run into a wall, don't turn around and give up. Figure out how to climb it, go through it, or work around it."*

~Michael Jordan

When I was playing baseball in high school, our coach gave everyone a packet conditioning folder with information to help us understand how to be successful baseball players. In the years since, I've realized that this manual teaches about life and about developing a mindset that can sustain you through just about anything – including a traumatic brain injury. Many of these concepts are now part of the principles that I live my life by today. I now share with you the philosophies and principles I have used to help live life as a brain injury survivor.

## My Mental Mission Statement

Being a professional baseball player had been my dream since I first picked up a baseball. I was well on my way and often wondered if I would have achieved my dream if I hadn't suffered a brain injury? I'll never know.

I attended Wheaton College to be their starting shortstop as a freshman. At that time, I didn't' think that anything could stop me. My goal had remained the same since I was six years old and I never stopped believing in myself. Since my injury, I have encountered many people along the way who actually told me to quit trying. Those who know me, however, know that I stick to what I believe. I know I can because no one knows what is best for me better than me. It is my life.

My mind remains focused on achieving my goals and getting to where I need to be. I was not brought back to life to do what others want me to do or what others think I should do. For me, anything is possible – anything. I just have to set my mind to it.

## Achieving Perspective

I now have a clear perspective on what I can and cannot do. I became a pitcher when I arrived at Wheaton College. It became clear that with my bad eyes and coordination it is harder for me to reach my dream. Rather than giving up, I simply found another dream. You are now part of my dream as my dream was t to write this book. It is my hope that I will truly inspire others who are down and need help to get back up.

These days, I now understand that I cannot drink alcohol. That is something my high school friends didn't understand. They thought I was no fun anymore because I couldn't do what they did. I have also become a different person in some ways and some can't accept that. That is one or the bigger reasons that I became closer with all of my home town friends after my brain injury. I am always comfortable around them because they have been truly lifelong and true friends. They understand and respect the situation I

[172]

am in. I will never forget what they have done for me since my accident.

## Personal Awareness

My life since my brain injury has offered me a better personal awareness about what to do so I can get to where I want to be. I stay away from all negativity and try to stay positive no matter what. Nothing could match the pain I have experienced since my coma, both physically and mentally. If people can't accept me for the way I am then that is their problem. This alone has set me free. You have to do the work and focus on yourself to get what you want. If the directions of things change you have to go with it and work with what you have. It's a simple concept that has changed my life for the better.

## Self-Motivation

Those who know me best know that I have always been self-motivated to work hard and win at everything that I do. The motivation I had was focused on the baseball field but is now focused on many other things. Okay, so maybe I won't be a professional baseball player. Today that is okay. I realized that I had to start focusing on other things. At first I created one goal – baseball. How other people judged me for the goals I created for myself means nothing. You can't listen to anyone but yourself because only you know what you can and cannot do. Self-awareness is important. Though they never realized it at the time, all the people who told me to quit only gave me more drive to move forward in my life. I did get on the baseball field, I did make it to college, and I did accomplish many things those people thought I wouldn't. It was my self-motivation that allowed me to achieve these important goals after my injury.

## Mental Discipline

I woke up from my coma and returned home to try to rebuild my life. I hadn't lost focus as my goal was same it was and has been my entire life. When people try to put me down, I don't listen to their negativity and like a balloon I let them fly away. They have not gone through and seen what I have so they don't know the determination I have gained from it. Those negative people and their negative thinking kept me down for many years but I learned to turn it into my own personal motivation. I will continue to go in the positive direction I am going for the rest of my life. There are no other options. Everyone must work hard to achieve their own personal dream no matter what they are told. From the obstacles that I have overcome I know I will keep moving in the right direction for the rest of my life. As my life has shown my, dreams may change but you must stay positive to get what you want.

## Self Confidence

Everyone needs confidence in themselves to find that determination to reach their goal. What can you do without confidence in yourself? Though this may sound strange to some, I have more self-confidence and I believe in myself more than I ever have. Any setback that puts you down, if find it in yourself to come back stronger than you were before, you have achieved success. Everyone has it in them and you know what you can do. If you have right mindset, there is nothing anyone can say to steer you in the wrong direction. I know today I can do anything I put my mind to.

## Competitive Intensity

I always had emotional control over myself when I was on the baseball diamond. This was because the skill I displayed did my talking for me. Yes, every player in any sport, at all levels has games or outings they are not proud of, as in life. They all have times they wished they performed better or didn't understand why they didn't do better.

With mental toughness, any subpar performance will make you work even harder so it doesn't happen again. My competitive intensity is always at its highest level. Everyone needs mental toughness and self-confidence to reach their goals. I use my competitive intensity every day to achieve my dream. It has never let me down.

## Team player

I have always had very good relationships with all of my teammates and coaches. There was never a time where I felt jealous of a teammate if they were performing better than I was. You need confidence in yourself as well as confidence in your teammates because that is what a team is about. Everyone on a team needs to work together for a common goal.

## Self-Esteem

I have always had high self-esteem but there were many days after my brain injury when I thought nothing of myself and that I would never get back to where I was. That feeling only propelled me to work harder.

Everyone needs high self-esteem. If you don't, you will let the pessimistic people in your life run your life for you. You have to remember that it is your life and your dream, no one else's. The positive feeling you have about yourself is the most important thing.

## Accountability

Sometimes my behaviors off the field have lead me into some trouble - but I never let it affect my performance on the baseball field. When I was on the diamond I was always focused on doing what is best for my team to win and best for me to reach my dream. No matter what your dream may be, you should focus and do what you must do to reach that dream.

[177]

## Continued Development

My social skills were lacking for many years after my coma. Some people couldn't accept what happened to me and didn't understand that I did some things now that I can't control. My athletic talents I always had control over. I never have to take responsibility for them. I was back on my feet in the middle of 2003 and knew what I had to do to get back to where I was going. That is determination. Without determination, you will never find your dreams.

## Chapter Nineteen

## Reengaging in Life

*"I'd like to be settled into somewhat of a normal life. Somewhat. I know it's never going to be completely normal. "*

~Michael Jordan

No matter how long it has been since my brain injury, I still meet and talk to people who can't and won't move on and leave the past in the past. Some friends of mine and some in my own family can't get by my mistake and let me live my life now how I want to. According to some, I now have to live a certain way and I can't do what I love anymore. That is just not going to happen. I believe in myself and believe I can do anything. I will not let anyone run my life for me. Those are the type of people I stay away from.

You need to feel good, be positive and don't let anyone to interrupt that.

By now, you know that I am a very stubborn person. If I could go back I would definitely change some of the things I said and the way I acted towards both my brother and sister over the years. I think they would change some of the things they said to me also. That is simply a sibling relationship. What's done is done and I honestly feel that our relationship has only become stronger. We are older now and appreciate what we do for one another more. That is all that matters. We have and continue to move forward.

Jackie, Don and their daughter Sara were three of my biggest supporters after my brain injury. They were there at the beginning and then every day for the next four years before I made it to Wheaton College. They kept me up during my worst days. Nicole, my ex-girlfriend, was their daughter too. Thankfully, even after we broke up, they were still there for me. Sara always kept my spirits up. I see her as one of my best friends. All three of them motivated me to keep doing what my heart pushes me to do.

They did so much for me and deserve much more than just a thank you.

When I got my license back, the first drive I took was over to visit them. Not only to say hello and talk with them but to thank them for everything they did to help me after my brain injury. What I really wanted to do was stop at the tree I hit and take a few chops at it with an ax. I realized however that part of my life is over and I can't go back. It only made me a stronger, more confident and determined person and athlete. Jackie, Don and Sara have become three of my best friends and I wouldn't change that for anything.

This part of my story is to say thank you to the three of them so they know I will remember and appreciate who they are and everything they did for me for the rest of my life. I first met them when I was at the top of the world. When I hit the bottom, they continued to be people I could count on. I am so happy I got the chance to get to know them before my brain injury because they played a huge role in my coming back. I know everything that happened, that happens to me every day and to any one is for a reason, for a purpose. I now see my brain injury the same way. I know I became close to them before, maybe for this reason: to be there for me when I needed someone the most. That is exactly what they did.

It is unfortunate that things went the way they did but I realized many years later how truly blessed I am to have them in my life. Maybe I was meant to suffer my brain injury. I now know I was meant to wake up and I am supposed to do what I am doing now - continuing to work on my dream and doing something that will change the way other people look at and live their lives.

My life is an open book. Feel free to look at me and what I have done. I am showing that with heart, dedication and determination almost anything is possible. However, if it wasn't for those who stayed by me, I wouldn't have come as far as I have or come close to play the game I love again. For many years, I would say to people, "Stop being you." Well, that changed. What I have to say to them is, "Thank you for being you and being you every day."

In 2011, I moved to Wakefield, Massachusetts. Because Wakefield was the third town I had moved to after my brain injury I knew it would be a good move. We all know that the third time is a charm. My mother and I moved to Wakefield to be closer to her boyfriend, Rich. I worked landscaping with Rich a few times a week and my mother really liked him. We worked for Supportive Living, which is a place that Rich had done a lot of volunteer work. He would take me and work with me. I got paid, he didn't. He is very good to my mother and me. He comes over to dinner every night and we kid around with each other. Without him I don't know where we would be.

The people in Wakefield are all very nice. So after moving from Topsfield to Middleton to Danvers to Wakefield, it looked like third time's a charm was really that. It was far enough away from everything that made me think about and reminded me of my brain injury. It helped me to really concentrate on myself. My best friend from my home town, Tim, moved here with his wife a year after I did.

Right across the street from us, there is a lake and baseball diamonds where I can still train. Activities like running around the lake and throwing my iron balls will improve my confidence and self-awareness. Exercise always helps me improve my outlook when I need an emotional lift or need to blow off some steam. A workout at the gym or a brisk 30-minute walk can help. Physical activity stimulates various brain chemicals that may leave you feeling happier and more relaxed. You may also feel better about your appearance and yourself when you exercise regularly, which can boost your spirit and improve your self-esteem. Some days I just don't want to go, but I make myself go because I know I will feel much better about my life afterwards.

Another benefit about my move to Wakefield was being near Dave. He is a good friend of mine that I went to high school with. He lives right down the street now. Dave was a grade ahead of me in high school but we played baseball together for several years. He was there every day in the hospital for me and continued his friendship with me when I came home. I know he was always there from the amount of pages of notes he wrote to me in my blue notebook I got when I left the hospital.

"When I heard about you being in the hospital I couldn't believe it, you're one of my best friends buddy and I would do anything for you."

I can't thank Dave enough for all he did for me before and after my brain injury. Like I said before, I didn't have many friends left but Dave kept his word and was always there. Thank you Dave.

Life is better with friends. No one is meant to go it alone in life. I met two people that I can call my best friends. I am lucky to have them as friends. I met Alex and Robin through a friend on Facebook. The first time I met Alex and Robin in person, I was in the hospital in 2012 getting my seizure medicine fixed. They came in to see me. They understand why I am the way I am and don't judge me for the little things I do that some people do judge me for. Alex and Robin have been so supportive and I can't thank them enough. I am lucky to have met people as nice and understanding as they are. Alex and Robin are people who will lead from the back to put others in front of them and lead the way. In the short time I have known them, they do so much for me. I will make sure to treasure their friendship in my life for as long as I live.

I have learned that when you are young it's wise not to take any relationship you have too seriously. That knowledge alone makes me feel wise beyond my years. Life is a long road to travel. I've learned that you will meet many and lose many people along the way - so there is no reason to think about the ones you have lost. It's all part of the journey. I do not regret any of the friendships or relationships I had because it was something I felt was right at the time.

Through life everyone goes through many different things but they are lessons learned along the way. You can't change what you did, but you can learn from the experiences that you go through. Girlfriends can be a big part of anyone's life, especially when you are young. Having Nicole leave me when I got home from the hospital was painful, but because I couldn't really remember our relationship, it wasn't that painful as it could have been. I just knew I liked having her around at a very low point in my life. As you get older you meet new people, get into new things, separate and change. It is just a part of life and something I learned, the hard way.

I didn't stay in contact with many old girlfriends from high school - except one. We were together my sophomore year but had a pretty hard break up. I sometimes thought about what happened between us but it seems she has forgotten all about it. Having her back to being a friend showed me something. I used to think that all people were bad. This was when I was stuck at home for so many years. I felt people are selfish and that they couldn't forgive and forget. She was someone who gave me a chance to show her what I could become.

Talking to her and getting to know her again was something I never thought would happen. I never thought a lot of things would happen that have over the course of my life and now I see that ANYTHING IS POSSIBLE. The drive and desire you have to achieve anything in life can be strong enough to overcome what some think is impossible, physical, mental or emotional.

Both of my parents have been there for me, not only from the start of my life but from the start of the hardest years of my life. I say that they both put me through hell after I woke up from my coma but it was my own doing. I am pretty sure that I put them through worse.

I can't imagine how they both felt that night. My father is the one who had me work with Annibal so I always thank him for that punishment. I tell him his punishment will be worse when I get my chance.

For years I let him know that I am going to send him to the Middleboro Greenery when he gets older because he did the same to me. His quick defensive response to me was always, "That was something your mother did." Either way, I tell him that Middleboro will be his new home and I will make sure that his roommate will be May. I know she would enjoy that and he can get all the hugs and kisses he wants.

I lived with my mother and didn't get to see my father as often as I would have liked - only when we go out to dinner, sometimes more. Because I lived with my mother, she got the worst of my grief and complaining, complaints about all the therapy I was doing, how much I hated it and I that wasn't it doing anymore. It took a while, but after many years I realized how much she sacrificed to help me. She does everything in her power to make my brother, sister and me happy. She is a one-of-a-kind mother and I am so happy I can say she is my mother.

I continue to question things regarding many aspects of my life. I wish I knew the answers, but I guess only time and experience will answer them for me. Everything I have been through since my brain injury taught me so much - who I am, things about the people in my life, the direction I am heading. I know today that I still have a lot to learn.

Since my coma, there have been people who attempted to tell me how to live my life. Now I have a different perspective on how to live and look at life. I found out a lot about the people who were the closest to me before that day. However that is in the past and I am only moving forward. I got my life back on track so I will be able to capture my dream. My experience really helped me grow as a person.

If I knew the things that I now know about certain people, my entire life would be different. Everyone knows who their friends are. It's natural to believe they will always be there for you if anything goes wrong. That is what a friend is supposed to be for. If you are in a hole, your friends will be there to pick you up. I believed that. I thought all my friends would be there for me through anything. I was mistaken. Some friends I had were just fair-weather friends. I will remember forever the friends of mine who stuck to their word and stayed with me.

I became the most positive person in the world after all I went through and I wouldn't change that for anything. Would I change what happened and wished it never did? My answer is, maybe.  For some reasons I would, but for others I wouldn't.  Either way I am now happy the way my life is going because of what I have gained and learned from my setback. That is all it was, a setback.  I believe in myself so I keep moving forward in a positive direction and that is how everyone should live and think, POSITIVE

# Chapter Twenty

## The Most Important Lesson in my Life

*"I want to be perceived as a guy who played his best in all facets, not just scoring. A guy who loved challenges. "*

~Michael Jordan

I wear a Rosary Bead necklace with a cross on it. This reminds me that where ever I am and whatever I am doing I have someone always looking out for me. One day I was at the gym in wearing them. Someone saw me with them on and said to me, "You know that you're not supposed to wear that kind of necklace, it's a sin."

His comment made me nervous so I asked my friend Father Mike about it. I told him what I was told and asked him if I should stop wearing the necklace. He laughed at my question and said, "No, it's not a sin, God likes when wear them because it shows your love and respect to him, don't listen to what other people say, you should wear them."

After he told me that, I felt much better and I don't listen to what other people say to me about them. I was getting ready for bed one night and pulled my shirt over my head and pulled the necklace off as well. A day later I realized I didn't have them on. I was so worried because I knew what the necklace meant and what it did for me. I asked Father Mike if he could get me another necklace like that because I thought I lost it mine. He said, "No I can't get you another one but don't worry, if you really want them back, God will get them back to you."

I felt better after he said that to me, but days went by and I still hadn't found them. It was about six days after he told me I would find them and I was cleaning my room for the second time. I picked up a pile of clothes off the floor and I heard something hit the ground. I looked down and there they were. I then looked to the sky and put my hands together and just said thank you. I talked to Father Mike a day later and told him I found them.

He said, "I told you, you would find them."

They could have been anywhere, in the wash or they could have fallen off in the swimming pool. When I got them back I knew someone was, has always been and I know will always be with me.

I pray every night because I know He hears me. I don't pray for myself because I feel that would be selfish. I pray for all of the people I have met since my accident who are in bad shape and I pray for the people I know in my life who need help. Every day and night, I look up and say thank you for what He has done me, for getting me back on the baseball field and helping me come so far. That is why I know I am not done. I feel that God has put me in His plan. I have a gift given from God so I am going to use it.

I know I was given a chance to show the reason I woke up and what I work so hard for. I thank God for my mother and my family being in my life. I ask God to keep helping Ronnie, my friend from Middleboro. I pray for everyone else that I met in all my rehabs over the years as well as for the people in my life who are having a hard time and for their families.

The power of prayer is more powerful than I ever thought before. I learned that lesson the hard way but

I did eventually learn it. I am only a better person today for it. This is the most important lesson I have learned since my coma. This is the most important lesson of my life.

I believe my life was saved by all the prayers for me when I was in my coma and years after. The events that have come to pass only made me stronger. I now see that all the things that tried to break me were the things that made me even stronger. I can't change the past because it is gone. I keep climbing the ladder and realize the past is just a series of lessons learned.

I was taught that I was saved by God and this is something I truly believe. When I left the Middleboro Greenery I began to think that if I was saved by God, why wouldn't He help all the other people there and the many more who I have met since 2002. If God saved me then why wouldn't He save them? Not why He wouldn't but why He couldn't. I know that some people are not religious so they might not understand what I am saying. You need to believe in yourself and work hard to get what you want. Someone opened my eyes, got me able to walk again, got me to college and got me ready to play the game I love at a higher level. I would not have called myself a religious man before my accident but now my views are much different because I feel I was given a second chance.

Today, I am dealing with my life in the present. I stopped worrying about the past because that's where it is, in the past. Every morning I wake up, look up and see the sun and it feels so good that I'm still here. I am not alone for a second. I have been taught and learned through my experience that if I believe in myself than there is nothing I can't do. Father Mike taught me so much not only what I can do, but what I can do with a strong belief in myself.

I encourage you to look at your life with new eyes. If you choose to look at your hardships as something that hold you back, you are destined to fulfill your belief. If, however, you choose to look at whatever hardship life throws at you with new eyes, you might just be amazed at what you see. I wish you peace and joy in your own life's journey and hope that by seeing how I have overcome seemingly insurmountable adversity, you can move forward with a new hope that inspires you to do your best – no matter what!

Made in the USA
Middletown, DE
01 June 2015